D0437647

Managing Health and Human Services Programs

A Guide for Managers

Stephen L. White

THE FREE PRESS
A Division of Macmillan Publishing Co., Inc.
NEW YORK

Collier Macmillan Publishers
LONDON

The Free Press
A Division of Macmillan Publishing Co., Inc.
866 Third Avenue, New York, N. Y. 10022

Collier Macmillan Canada, Ltd.

Library of Congress Catalog Card Number: 80–1057

Printed in the United States of America

printing number
1   2   3   4   5   6   7   8   9   10

Quote by Sheila D. Melville from *Smith College School for Social Work Journal*, 1978, 5(1): 2–5. Reprinted by permission of the author.
Quote by Gail Thain Parker from *The Atlantic Monthly*, copyright © 1976 by the Atlantic Monthly Company. Reprinted by permission of the author.
Quote by E. B. White from *The Points of My Compass*, copyright © 1962 by Harper & Row Publishers, Inc. Reprinted by permission.
Quote by Ralph Littlestone from *The Administration of Mental Health Services*, edited by Saul Feldman, copyright © 1973 by Charles C. Thomas, Publisher. Reprinted by permission.

Library of Congress Cataloging in Publication Data

White, Stephen L
  Managing health and human services programs.

  Includes index.
  1. Social work administration.   2. Health
services administration.   3. Middle managers,
Training of.   I. Title.   [DNLM: 1. Services--Or-
gan.   2. Social work--Organ.   W84.1 W588m]
HV41.W47 1981   361'.0068   80-1057
ISBN 0-02-934550-2

To
Lawrence and Claire White,
  who taught me how to manage myself,
and
Jodi and Christen White,
  with whom I manage nicely.

CONTENTS

PREFACE

Professionals in the human services who have clinical or technical backgrounds are often bewildered and lost when they are promoted to management positions. As befits their many years of education, they turn to the literature for help in learning the language and skills of management that are so new to them. And what do they find? They find, first, a vast corpus of research, articles, and books from business and industry that begins to answer only some of their questions. But, the goals and methods of human services management are different in many ways from those of business management. Second, when they turn to the human services literature, they find a much smaller and more recent body of writings, directed principally to chief executives of human services agencies. These works, too, offer some help. But new middle managers in the human services soon grow discouraged in their search for journals and books that address their unique needs and experiences as novices in the world of management. It is for them that I wrote this book.

This book is addressed to those professionals who have recently become, or aspire to be, managers in social work, psychology, nursing, education, medicine, and related disciplines. It begins by introducing the new or aspiring manager to the many difficulties inherent in making the transition from clinician to manager. A clinical manager in charge of a small program or department in a clinic, school, hospital, or agency is a *middle* manager in many senses. The most problematic, at least in the beginning, is the sense in which the clinical manager feels pulled from one side by his identity as a clinician and from the other side by his emerging identity as a manager, roles that seem at first to be irreconcilable. The feeling of being pulled from both sides rarely ever goes away entirely. But one *can* emerge from the confusion, relatively undaunted, with some idea of the similarities between clinical work and management, as well as an idea of precisely how they differ.

After addressing the general area of managerial role transition, this book attempts to cover some of the essential aspects of a human services manager's job and to provide basic information necessary to function effectively in the new role. One can think of the book as divided into two parts, moving from the general to the specific aspects of human services management. The first half deals with such broad areas as organizational theory, leadership, decisionmaking, communication, and, as already mentioned, general issues in becoming a manager. The second half of the book takes up some of the specific tasks of management: planning, budgeting and finance, productivity, program evaluation, and personnel management. Each chapter seeks to introduce the reader to basic concepts in each area through a review of classic and recent literature and through a practical discussion of workable techniques.

This book is meant to be a primer and nothing more. It is not meant to be an exhaustive or comprehensive review of the literature. Nor does it cover all the practical aspects of human services management. For example, the chapter on budgeting and finance purposely omits much that an experienced manager would want to know. What it does do, however, is to introduce this topic to those who may never before have prepared or monitored a budget. It contains very little accounting jargon but presents a foundation upon which a new middle manager in the human services can build. All of the topics covered are treated in a similar manner.

A few threads that run through this book should be highlighted from the outset. These threads reveal basic assumptions that are useful to a manager in the human services. The first is that social organizations are composed of many interdependent and dynamically interacting parts such that a change in one part sets off changes in other parts. This idea is called "systems theory" and it is useful in explaining and understanding how organizations work. The second assumption is that it is a manager's job to integrate the various parts of his organization so that they work in harmony with each other. Furthermore, a manager must insure that his organization fits into a broader system of human services organizations so that duplication of effort is avoided and interorganizational cooperation is enhanced. The third assumption that runs through this book is that organizations exist for specific purposes and human services organizations exist to benefit their consumers. The goals and objectives of a human services organization, therefore, should constantly be the manager's guide in his work.

Another set of assumptions guided this book and its author. First, I believe that *clinicians* are best suited to run human services organizations but only after having acquired the skills necessary to be managers. Second, I regard management as both a useful and a tremendously rewarding endeavor. Few accomplishments are as gratifying as the successful orchestration of staff, technology, and other resources in a program designed to benefit people.

ACKNOWLEDGMENTS

The saying that writing is a lonely endeavor is only partially true. Although I am solely responsible for any shortcomings in this work, I owe a great debt to many people who helped me transform rough ideas and scribblings into something coherent and, I hope, useful. My greatest debt is to my friend and colleague Dr. Anthony Broskowski, who first encouraged me to write this book and who has given freely of his time to review and criticize each chapter. I am grateful for all his help. I am also indebted to Dr. Patricia Ewalt, who read and carefully commented on the entire manuscript. I was indeed fortunate to have had such an insightful, perceptive, and thorough reviewer to give me advice. Ron Chambers, my editor at The Free Press, is the kind of editor every author would like to have but few get. He maintained his enthusiasm for this project from the beginning, even when my own faltered. He also gave encouragement and advice that I could not have done without and, in the process, became a friend. Dr. Dwight Harshbarger, Ron Ravneberg, and Jodi White also made many useful editorial comments on early drafts.

Many of the ideas and examples in this book come from my own experiences as a human services manager. My thoughts and experiences have been greatly influenced by my relationships with colleagues and friends at the Court Clinic of the Cambridge-Somerville Community Mental Health Center in Massachusetts and at St. Joseph's Hospital, the University of South Florida College of Medicine, and Northside Community Mental Health Center in Tampa. I am especially grateful to Jo Gorman, Dr. Gary Wood, Nancy Lester, and Dr. Robert Fernandez for many useful suggestions and comments. A special word of thanks is due to Maryann Austin, my superb secretary, who typed and typed and typed!

And finally, if it had not been for the constant understanding, support, and encouragement of my wife, Jodi, there would have been no book at all.

1 On Becoming a Manager

It is a commonplace in the technical and service delivery fields that those line workers who perform best are in due course promoted to supervisory and management positions in the organization, even though it is known that the best line workers do not necessarily make the best managers. Although there are similarities, management requires skills and ways of viewing work environments different from those of line work. This dilemma is often the cause of conflict both within the organization and within the professional become manager. This chapter will examine how organizations choose managers and how professionals choose to become, and then *do* become, managers. Next the chapter will discuss some of the problems related to taking over the management of a work group. Finally, the chapter will present some comments about preparing oneself to become a manager.

The terms "manager," "middle manager," and "clinical manager" will be used interchangeably. In the human services middle managers are those whose responsibilities include administrative duties as well as technical work. They are the first line of supervisors, one step removed from consumers by direct service workers. Middle managers in human services agencies are a head nurse on a surgical ward, the chairman of the English department in a public high school, the chiefs of social work and psychology in a traditional child guidance center, the supervisor of a unit of vocational rehabilitation counseling, and the chief dietician in a general hospital. Other examples abound. These professionals, with varied technical backgrounds, have much in common. They must insure that quality services for people are delivered efficiently in an everchanging environment of government regulations, consumer activism, and budget limitations. They are responsible for hiring staff, monitoring worker schedules and productivity, arbitrating staff conflicts, monitoring the effectiveness of the services being offered, supervising the technical work of professional and nonprofessional subordi-

1

nates, and interacting with other managers in their own organization and with others in the community. Throughout this book the word "clinical" is used to modify the term "manager." Clinical is used in the most general sense to denote that which concerns the direct delivery of human services. A clinical manager, such as a chief physical therapist, is thus set apart from an administrative manager, such as a personnel department director.

ACCEPTING A MANAGEMENT ROLE

Top management in the human services rarely recruit managers whose only background is management or business. People chosen to be middle managers usually have demonstrated special knowledge, skills, or abilities in some field other than management or supervision. The supervisor in a family services agency is generally a senior social worker. Similarly, it is difficult to imagine a manager of a community mental health center's outpatient clinic who lacks professional training or experience in doing psychotherapy. Clearly, there are advantages to picking the best technicians to be supervisors. Experienced technicians and clinicians have great empathy for the overworked, underpaid human service worker. They also are familiar with the type of services being provided and presumably know how to insure high quality service for the client. These experienced clinical supervisors are best suited to orient and train new professionals who enter the organization. The manager and his subordinates must work toward goals they all understand and accept, openly communicating with each other along the way.

What else, besides clinical and technical expertise, should make the professional service provider a good choice for a supervisory position? A person who has shown in his professional work a high degree of enthusiasm, initiative, and imagination, as well as maturity and good judgment. Also, the ability to get along with others is crucial for a manager. These are a few of the personal qualities, along with common sense and a sense of humor, that make people good leaders. There is another quality of good managers that should not be overlooked but often is: intellectual curiosity. A curious or questioning person will not be satisfied with simple solutions to complex problems and will work hard to understand the complexities of the work environment.

Another quality of good managers is the ability to communicate clearly and to view the organization as a whole. The first of these, communication, involves not only the ability to express ideas orally in a clear, concise manner but also the ability to write lucid letters and memoranda to superiors, subordinates, and consumers. An inability to communicate orally and in writing will limit the impact that a manager's new ideas and plans have on an organization. What is worse, poor communication may lead to confusion, low morale, and inferior services. The ability to view the organization as a whole is essential so that the manager's efforts will harmonize with wider organizational goals and with the efforts of other managers. One must continually be aware of the ways that events in one program or department have important ripple effects in other parts of the organization. In this respect, a manager must shift his focus from the individual client or worker to the broader perspective of the total organization. This change in focus may be made more difficult in a large organization by a new manager's loyalties to old friends in the component in which he first worked.

A manager must also be able to make decisions that reflect the service goals of the organization. Moreover, he must be able to mediate conflicts between and among staff, clients, or other managers, and governing board members.

This brief list is representative of what sets one professional apart from another in terms of ability to make the transition from service provider to supervisor.

What is it that attracts a clinician to management? After a few years of caring for patients, teaching, or providing other kinds of direct services, a professional begins to look for ways to advance within the system. The first opportunities to present themselves usually concern quasi-administrative duties of a limited nature or perhaps the supervision of graduate students. Although private practice or further education are possible options for some, it is difficult to advance within the human services delivery system, especially if one conceives of advancement as meaning increased salary or higher status. As Melville (1978) pointed out, "Annual merit increases come and go, year after year, and then they slow up, so the system itself prods [the clinician] on or does not reward her financially for staying-put, or staying-put at the same level of responsibility, and there is the rub. She realizes that she is not being financially rewarded for being *just* a good clinician" (p. 2). Added to the allure of higher pay is the attraction of higher status within the organization.

It is perhaps not too sweeping a generalization to suggest that human services professionals are somewhat competitive and probably rate higher than average in achievement motivation. Sarason (1972) has pointed out that most children have fantasies of being powerful in the service of others; powerful heroes in current events and in the media are idealized. Sarason goes on to note that as the child grows older he is no longer rewarded for his fantasies of power, and modesty becomes an inhibitory force. Society reinforces the ideal of the selfless and altruistic leader: "Whereas custom requires that the leadership fantasy be expressed as an opportunity to do good for others, phenomenologically the individual does not experience his striving only in such virtuous ways" (p. 190). Guilt is frequently the product of the split between public altruism and private selfishness and is diminished over time, usually by the satisfaction of private needs in keeping with the interests of the public. The guilty tension is exacerbated by the conscious self-image of most human services professionals as that of a "nice guy" who is loath to exercise power (Klerman, 1974). One cannot get around the fact, however, that managers have power, no matter how limited. The problem of power will be discussed in greater length in a later chapter. In the meantime, though, we would do well to recognize the attraction that increased power has for most of us, however illicit we may feel that attraction is.

Finally, clinicians are attracted to management because of the inherent satisfactions in managerial work. Although there are many problems to be faced as a manager, the problems can be challenges to a person's creativity, initiative, and intellect. Successfully meeting these challenges can be tremendously satisfying.

ROLE TRANSITION

When a professional shows management potential and is offered a promotion, he must undergo a radical change in role. A role change may necessitate substantial changes in self-image. Since self-image is often linked to self-esteem, the change may, and usually does, produce stress and tension at home and at work. Hirschowitz (1974) stated that when people pass into a new role they lose what they have been accustomed to in their old role. They lose familiar ties that have helped them maintain their equilibrium and internal harmony. As one leaves an old role and is not yet settled into a new role, one is in limbo and quite vulnerable to stress. Loss, grief, and mourning, under various guises and of varying intensities, are inevitable in periods of role transition. For these reasons, it is generally unwise to undergo several role changes, such as marriage and a job promotion, at the same time.

The stress and grief that accompany a role change from direct service work to middle management are predictable and resolvable phenomena. They are however, aggravated by the need to acquire technical skills: new managers must learn about spans of control, productivity evaluations, budgets, and other things that read like a management science litany. Levinson and Klerman (1967), in a now classic paper on the clinician-executive, catalogued seven "problematic role-tasks" that they argued must be negotiated by the new manager in order to achieve what they called a "clinician-executive synthesis." These seven role-tasks will now be briefly defined and discussed.

Developing an Integrated Social-Psychological Conception of the Organization and its Societal Context

This is usually a difficult task to accomplish, especially for the human services professional trained in the psychology of the individual. The clinician has a great deal of knowledge and experience that have prepared him to interact with, and provide services to, individuals. Some professionals, family therapists, and community organizers, for example, are trained to understand social systems and how they function. But even these professionals must develop an understanding of formal organizational theory and the ways in which individuals and large, complex organizations interact in work and political settings (for an excellent treatment of this subject written specifically for practitioners see Demone, 1978). The natural temptation to view "organizational problems solely in terms of the particular situations and individuals involved, and to overlook the more fundamental difficulties in the character of the organization itself" must be avoided (Levinson and Klerman, 1967, p. 7).

Becoming a Social System Clinician

All of the role-tasks that follow, including becoming a social system clinician, involve action as opposed to the intellectual and attitudinal change required by the first role-task. Levinson and Klerman suggested that the middle manager "treats" a social system rather than a family or an individual. He must maintain the system and keep it (or make it) "healthy" by such strategies as phasing out obsolete programs, hiring new people, firing some, shifting budgetary priorities, or inspiring the staff.

Dealing with Other Staff Members: The Problem of Authority

In any organization the middle manager has at least three levels of co-workers with whom he must deal: superiors, colleagues on the same hierarchical level, and subordinates. While there are commonalities in the ways that the middle manager will relate to all of these groups, there are important differences, too. Even though many human services organizations place a high value on democratizing their staffs, the power issues inherent in relating to these three groups are still present. In fact, as Levinson and Klerman thoughtfully pointed out, the flattening of the hierarchy may serve to complicate power issues by obscuring them.

Negotiation is a key word in developing this role-task. The middle manager must negotiate with a variety of individuals and groups in order to be effective. "Whenever people exchange ideas with the intention of changing relationships, whenever they confer for agreements, they are negotiating" (Nierenberg, 1973, p. 4). This is an area where clinical and executive skills merge (see Demone, 1978).

Finally, the new middle manager must learn how to exercise authority over subordinates in a way that achieves organizational goals and encourages and supports the professional and nonprofessional staff. Subordinates are the most important constituency of the middle manager: without their support he will find his effectiveness limited. Sometimes the manager must exercise ultimate authority by firing someone who may be harmful to fellow workers or to the whole organization (this problem will be discussed in Chapter 10).

Relating to Other Mental Health Professionals and Disciplines

When a person enters a profession he is socialized into a way of viewing himself and develops a loyalty and dedication to the profession. He sees himself as a psychologist or a social worker or a nurse. Sometimes professional allegiances become barriers among different professional groups. Managers in modern human services systems must deal with people from a variety of professional backgrounds and orientations in a way that respects what each person and profession has to offer the organization. In this regard, the useless, and sometimes destructive, elitism of advanced education and certain professional and academic orientations must be avoided (Yessian and Broskowski, 1977, argued that we are entering an era of generalists, especially in human services administration).

Dealing with Persons, Groups, and Institutions outside One's Organization

This role-task has to do with a middle manager's impact on his organization's "outputs" into the community. Output refers to an organization's transformation of resources into products (Katz and Kahn, 1978). The middle manager must be concerned not only with the quantity of output but also with quality. These are two areas that are gaining in importance as governmental agencies and agency boards demand proof that scarce dollars are having maximum effect in terms of numbers of units of service and outcome of the service. Middle managers must learn new skills to orchestrate resources to achieve these ends. He must also become familiar, more than in a passing way, with the emerging fields of information systems, needs assessment, and program evaluation (see Attkisson, Hargreaves, Horowitz, and Sorenson, 1978).

In addition to monitoring inputs (resources) and outputs (products), the middle manager must learn to negotiate with other groups in the community. For example, the managers of all the community mental health center emergency services in an urban area must be able to negotiate territory and resources so that persons in acute emotional distress can get immediate help near their homes at any time. These managers must also know how to deal with police and ambulance officials, hospital emergency ward nurses, and a host of other people who manage the array of human services available (or, alas, not available) in a given area on a twenty-four-hour basis. As Demone

(1978) cautioned "The ultimate objective and the one which usually has the best potential is a negotiation which has both sides winning. Of course you may want to gain more than your opponent; but, if you plan to be in the arena again, you should avoid having your opponent lose public face" (p. 82).

Finally, the middle manager must be concerned with public relations not only for his service area or department but for the entire organization. The public's understanding of a service affects future funding and community use of the service. It is important to create a constituency that will support the services of the organization if they come under the scrutiny of regulatory or funding agencies.

Providing for Organizational Growth and Innovation

Organizations must be able to change and develop to avoid stagnation and to respond to the miltiple agencies and constituencies that have some say in how a human services agency is run. The middle manager must both respond to the demands of change and produce change by presenting ideas to superiors and by challenging staff to do new things or old things in new ways. This calls for flexibility, initiative, and a high tolerance for ambiguity as well as the ability to handle the strains of a constantly changing work environment. While change is vital to the organization, the middle manager must be aware that continuous change is usually destructive and organizations need periods of stability in order to consolidate changes that have been made and to regroup resources for future change (Broskowski, Mermis, and Khajavi, 1975).

Achieving the New Identity of Clinician-Executive

This section on role transition began with an allusion to self-image; professional socialization was also mentioned. This last role-task is an extension of these issues. A new identity is not an easy thing to acquire (ask any adolescent or newly married or retired person). After a professional has been a manager for sufficient time to have fought and survived some of the inevitable battles, there comes a time when he pauses to ask himself, "Is this what I went to graduate school for?" If the answer is no, then he should go back to direct service, teaching, private practice, or consulting. If, on the other hand, the answer is yes he must expect some of the feelings mentioned earlier that accompany major developmental transitions. A yearning for the days when life was simple and direct service was one's work is not uncommon. Loneliness, depression, feelings of insecurity, short-temperedness, insomnia, inexplicable headaches and stomach pains, and other signs of stress and anxiety are commonly experienced by new managers. These problems often diminish with time and in direct proportion to the extent that the new manager can honestly discuss his acute discomfort with co-workers, friends, and family members.

The clinician turned manager must be able to take a realistic look at the similarities of service delivery and management. Qualities of firmness and initiative and the ability to set goals and limits and take decisive action at crucial times are important both to service delivery *and* to management. As the professional internalizes this overlapping of two separate identities, he begins to form a new synthesis of the two. The differences and similarities of direct service work and managerial work will be apparent throughout the remainder of this book.

Managers in the human services experience another kind of strain common to all professionals in the human services. It is mentioned here because the manager not only will have to deal with it himself but also will have to be aware of it in order to supervise subordinates. I am referring to the dilemmas faced by professionals working in organizations. It has long been a characteristic of professionals that they determine how to apply their special knowledge and skills with a great deal of autonomy. It is very difficult, however, to maintain professional identity and autonomy in human services organizations, which even with the best management are bureaucratic and responsible to citizen boards as well as to federal, state, and local regulatory and funding bodies. For example, if state regulations and local funding agencies require a community mental health center to see a high volume of clients, then group therapy and planned short-term therapy will of necessity be the major modalities of treatment. These constraints may run counter to the therapists' professional judgment that long-term, insight-oriented psychotherapy is the only way to care for most patients. The middle manager represents the bureaucracy and its authority. Therefore, he often must mediate between the professional line workers on the one hand and top management on the other hand. This conflict is exacerbated by his own feelings of being a pawn in a game he cannot control. For an excellent treatment of this issue see Sarason (1977) and especially his painful discussion of job dissatisfaction among professionals in community mental health centers.

THE PROBLEM OF SUCCESSION

Most new middle managers assume responsibility for preexisting departments or other organizational structures. Whether promoted from within or recruited from outside the organization, a professional taking over the management of a work group will face problems related to the attitudes and expectations of subordinates that are at least as difficult to weather as the clinician-executive dilemma described earlier. Usually, the first manifestation of the problem of succession is a vague sense of loneliness at work. This loneliness stems from the new manager's inability to gain access to the informal network of the work group. An important part of the informal network is the well-known office grapevine, the source of a vast amount of important information about who's who and how to get things done in the organization as well as the real reasons things are done as they are. The informal network is also a communication network by which all manner of covert messages about what is acceptable and what is not acceptable to ingroup members are transmitted.

More will be said about formal and informal groups in later chapters. For the present discussion we must turn our attention to the effects of a new middle manager's inability to use the informal network. One effect is that the manager may greatly offend subordinates or make embarrassing mistakes because of a lack of information about the possible impact his actions or intended actions may have. For example, one may write an official-sounding memorandum to subordinates directing them to change a certain procedure. However, if they respond best when they are orally asked to make changes in an informal manner during staff meetings, the new directive is likely to meet with unexpected and unspoken resistance. Another effect of the new manager's isolation is increased use of the formal, bureaucratic system. Since the new manager has no other avenues open to him he may decide to "go by the book" (Gouldner, 1954), but the greater reliance on formality may further alienate the old guard and prolong the new manager's isolation.

Even if the middle manager has been promoted from within the organization this isolation is very likely to occur. The clear message from former co-workers is "you're one of *them* now." The new manager may respond by aligning himself with the administration or by assuring former peers that he will be their advocate no matter what. Even though a neutral stance is safer, and in the long run more productive, whatever position one takes is likely to be misinterpreted. Recently a new administrative assistant in a large general hospital related his experience in this regard. He had spent a year in the hospital as an administrative intern prior to becoming employed as an administrative assistant. During his year as a student he had enjoyed a very friendly relationship with most of the head nurses in the hospital. He was offered an administrative position when he graduated and everything suddenly changed. "It was like I wasn't the same person," he said. "I *feel* like the same person I always was, but now they treat me differently. They don't ask me to have coffee with them anymore. And they call me *Mr.* Munson instead of Jack like they used to."

Another important factor in succession is what Gouldner (1954) dubbed the "Rebecca myth." The reference is to the novel by Daphne DuMaurier about a young woman who married a widower. His first wife, Rebecca, was apparently idealized by the man and her memory plagued his new bride because she could never seem to measure up to Rebecca. Gouldner studied the succession of a new manager in a gypsum plant whose previous manager had been immensely popular. The previous manager's "old lieutenants" did not transfer their loyalty to the new manager and were "strategically replaced."

Hodgson, Levinson, and Zeleznik (1965) discovered instances in which new managers were idealized because of the unpopularity of previous managers. Kotin and Sharif (1974) consequently suggested that the Rebecca myth be expanded to include both negative and positive responses to new managers. Furthermore, negative and positive reactions to a new manager can exist simultaneously in the same organization.

During a time of initial social isolation the new manager may be approached by subordinates offering friendship and loyalty. The temptation to be taken in by these overtures is great and most times it is quite safe to respond in kind. It is important, however, to guard against the occasional insincere worker who curries the new manager's favor with his own selfish and counterorganizational ends in mind. The new manager should take the time to get to know all of his subordinates and to assert his own leadership style and identity before responding too warmly to friendly staff members. This rather Machiavellian stance will allow the manager greater latitude in interpersonal relations after he becomes "settled in" and will obviate awkward retreats from sycophants.

GETTING OVER THE HUMP

The process of conceiving of oneself as a manager is a difficult one, just as it is difficult to take over a management position someone else has held. The hardest thing about being a middle manager, though, is being in the middle. To bear responsibility for the quotidian functioning of the work group as well as larger administrative and organizational concerns is at best burdensome and at worst confusing. The middle manager must interpret policies and directives to the staff from top management and give top management information about what is going on with staff members and their programs. A good illustration of this concerns the coordinator of a psychiatric day hospital who once related that his staff devised a new plan for screening prospective patients. It was a plan that called for some major changes in the program and had to be cleared with the mental health center's executive. When the coordinator presented a draft proposal to the executive, the executive rejected the plan, giving many reasons why it was impracticable. Frustrated by his experience of being caught in the middle, this young coordinator said that when his staff had first presented the plan it had sounded not only reasonable but beyond any possible objection. But when he presented the plan to the executive, he found the executive's objections equally reasonable and well founded. "I didn't know what to think. I agreed with the staff *and* the director, but they didn't agree with each other!''

This vignette captures the essence of being a middle manager with all its pains. To survive the new middle manager can do several things. First he must find a mentor. He should meet regularly with an experienced manager in order to discuss ideas, thoughts, feelings, and conflicts about his new role. If there are problems with superiors within his own organization, he should find a mentor in another organization. If he cannot find such an advisor, then the new middle manager should arrange to have weekly meetings with other middle managers from other human services agencies. This informal support group will help him maintain a more realistic perspective on daily battles and tribulations.

Another survival strategy that is easier to discuss than to implement is the practice of recruiting one's own staff. Sarason (1972) referred to this as forming the ''core group,'' the new leader's ''chosen.'' Members of the organization who are hired by the new leader have none of the intraorganizational loyalties that older members may have and are thereby better able to help implement the new manager's ideas and programs. The difficulty with this strategy is twofold. First, the manager may be constrained by budget, personnel policies, unattractive fringe benefits, or a slow attrition rate in being able to recruit new staff. Second, as Sarason pointed out, the manager may have unrealistically high expectations about the caliber of staff he is able to recruit and may be sorely disappointed when he finds that he must settle for far less than he had hoped for. Nevertheless, over time a manager will usually be able to surround himself with staff with whom he feels comfortable.

The relationship between the middle manager and his superior is also crucial to his survival in the organization. The new middle manager must gain a clear understanding of the priorities and philosophies of his superior early in their relationship. The new manager must develop a cordial relationship with his boss so that a sense of mutual respect and trust is promoted. Also, the new manager should negotiate an understanding with the boss so that each is clear about how much autonomy and authority the new middle manager is to have. The manager must know whether, and under what circumstances, his superior will back him.

Because most human services managers have a clinical or service background, the new manager should seek out educational opportunities to begin to learn more about the art and technology of management. Many organizations and universities offer formal and informal seminars and courses in management theory and practice (see the Appendix).

Perhaps we have paid too much attention to the vexations of management and not enough to the rewards. That is not because the troubles outweigh the rewards. Although the problems are more apparent to the beginning manager, the pleasure that one receives from being instrumental in the development and management of a well-run service delivery system, watching staff grow professionally, and experimenting with new organizational strategies can be great.

Professional caregivers must be willing to fill middle management positions when they become open. For, as Dressler (1978) rightly noted, if we are unwilling to manage, then we may face a future in service systems led "by nonclinician bureaucratic administrators who may be more accountable to monolithic institutions than to the health care professionals or to the consumer population that they serve" (p. 360). As Dressler implies, professionals are as much a constituency of the manager as are consumers. The following chapter will be concerned with the ways that the manager can maximize the resources of the first constituency for the mutual benefit of both.

REFERENCES

ATTKISSON, C. C., HARGREAVES, W. A., HOROWITZ, M. J., AND SORENSON, J. E. *Evaluation of Human Service Programs*. New York: Academic, 1978.

BROSKOWSKI, A., MERMIS, W. L., AND KHAJAVI, F. "Managing the dynamics of change and stability." In J. E. Jones and J. W. Pfeiffer (eds.), *The 1975 Annual Handbook for Group Facilitators*. LaJolla, California: University Associates, 1975.

DEMONE, H. W. "Stimulating human services reform." *Human Services Monograph Series*, number 8, Washington, D.C.: Project Share, June 1978.

DRESSLER, D. M. "Becoming an administrator: the vicissitudes of middle management in mental health organizations." *American Journal of Psychiatry* (1978) 135(3):357–360.

GOULDNER, A. W. *Patterns of Industrial Bureaucracy*. New York: Free Press, 1954.

HIRSCHOWITZ, R. G. "Role transition and psychological cost accounting." Paper presented at the conference "The Human Service Leader as an Agent of Change: Strategies and Dilemmas" sponsored by the Human Resource Institute of Boston, Chestnut Hill, March 27, 1974.

HODGSON, R. C., LEVINSON, D., AND ZELEZNIK, A. *The Executive Role Constellation*. Boston: Division of Research, Harvard Business School, 1965.

KATZ, D., AND KAHN, R. L. *The Social Psychology of Organizations*. 2d edition. New York: Wiley, 1978.

KLERMAN, G. "The joys and vicissitudes of life as a clinician-executive." Paper presented at the conference "The Human Service Leader as an Agent of Change: Strategies and Dilemmas" sponsored by the Human Resource Institute of Boston, Chestnut Hill, March 26, 1974.

KOTIN, J., AND SHARIF, M. R. "Management succession and administrative style." *Administration in Mental Health*. (1974) 3(4):46–49.

LEVINSON, D., AND KLERMAN, G. "The clinician-executive: some problematic issues for the psychiatrist in mental health organizations." *Psychiatry* (1967) 30 (1):3–15.

MELVILLE, S. D. " 'Do you like your job?' Personal reflections of a clinical-manager." *Smith College School for Social Work Journal* (1978) 5(1):2–5.

NIERENBERG, G. I. *Fundamentals of Negotiating.* New York: Hawthorn, 1973.

SARASON, S. B. *The Creation of Settings and the Future Societies.* San Francisco: Jossey-Bass, 1972.

_____. *Work, Aging, and Social Change.* New York: Free Press, 1977.

YESSIAN, M. R., AND BROSKOWSKI, A. "Generalists in human-service systems; their problems and prospects." *Social Service Review* (1977) 51(2):265–288.

2 The Organizational Context

A colleague once told me of the ingenious way a middle level manager in a county health department in California handled the flood of paper that daily came into his office demanding immediate attention. All the papers and letters he received during the week would be placed in a folder marked "1." Each Monday morning he would take the previous week's file and place it in a file marked "2," the previous week's "2" file in a file marked "3," and so on until after six weeks a letter or document would end up in a file marked "6." This man worked only on papers that had been aged for six weeks unless he received a call from a superior asking him what was happening with a particular letter or memorandum. In such cases, the manager would immediately attend to the project that his superior had just asked about. It will come as no surprise that fully 60 percent of the papers aged for six weeks no longer warranted anyone's attention. These papers were placed in the terminal file of this simple system, the wastebasket, and were not missed.

This story, although it sounds apocryphal, is nevertheless representative of some people's response—and adaptation—to large bureaucratic organizations that generate an endless stream of memoranda, seemingly useless paperwork, and cold, impersonal messages. Organizational structures are a fact of life and the middle manager must understand them in order to make working in them as pleasant and productive as possible. Before going on, though, I must point out that not all organizations are insensitive, monolithic, and absurd. They certainly may be all those terrible things, but they don't have to be. Many top managers in the human services are truly interested in making their organizations responsive to the human needs of their clients and employees by diminishing, as much as possible, all that is onerous and superfluous. Middle managers, as well, can do much to humanize the organizations in which they work.

14

Perhaps one reason why professionals chafe in organizations is that the service providers are naturally incompatible with other parts of the organization in ways that most organizational theory does not explain. Organizational theory is borrowed largely from business and industry and describes organizations that exist for the benefit of their owners. Human services organizations are different from business and industrial concerns in two important ways. First, human services organizations exist to serve consumers whose needs are supposed to be paramount. Second human services organizations are closely governed by citizens, some of whom may be consumers. These two points, in addition to the preponderance of professionals in human services organizations, make them quite different from business and industrial structures. We shall examine these differences later in this chapter. Now we will begin our examination of organizations with an overview of the historical roots of organizational theory.

AN OVERVIEW

Traditional organizational theories are concerned primarily with the internal structures of the organization, which dictated a closed-system approach to organizational problems. A closed-system approach considers factors outside the boundary of the organization either irrelevant or far less important than internal factors in the life of the organization. An open-system approach, conversely, takes into account the flow of information, resources, and products between the organization and its external environment. Modern organizational theory is based upon an open-system approach. Before considering the open-system model, however, we shall briefly examine four traditional notions about social organizations that predate the current open-system approach.

The first theory to consider is that of Max Weber (1864–1920), who was concerned with the legitimization and formalization of roles within organizations. Weber is well known for his description of bureaucracy—as he called it, "rational-iegal bureaucracy." The modifier "rational-legal" is crucial because it implies that bureaucratic organizations should be deliberate and rational in approaching their goals. This important contribution is evident in Weber's list of essential components of the rational-legal bureaucracy:

- Hierarchy of positions with each lower position under the control of a higher one.
- Division of labor whereby specialists perform special tasks.
- Uniformly written rules for performing all organizational functions.
- Impersonality whereby all members of the organization are subject to formal rules of conduct and follow these rules in their interactions.

• Specialists and other workers are assigned to their positions by virtue of their competence and not their political contacts or social class.

In elaborating on his description of this form of organization Weber (1964) wrote:

> It is superior to any other form in precision, in stability, in the stringency of its discipline, and in its reliability. It thus makes possible a particularly high degree of calculability of results for the heads of organization and for those acting in relation to it. It is finally superior both in intensive efficiency and in the scope of its operations, and is formally capable of application to all kinds of administrative tasks.

Although Weber's bureaucracy is far from complete by today's standards, especially in terms of an organization's interchange with its environment, it forms the foundation for many contemporary organizational designs and theories. Certainly, the components of the rational-legal bureaucracy are common to most organizations, including organizations that espouse an open-system approach; even open systems require some degree of role definition and internal uniformity.

The next two organizational theories concern themselves with the practical problems of organizing a work group for efficient functioning. The first, Frederick W. Taylor's (1856–1915) approach to shop management, applies what later was called "scientific management" to the bureaucratic organization. The cornerstone of Taylor's contribution to management is "orderliness"; he developed methods to organize routine work procedures according to findings from time and motion studies. Although Taylor was concerned about working conditions and attempted to improve them through specialization and rationality in the workplace, scientific management, for the sake of historical perspective, is usually considered a task-oriented view of management. It is a view particularly well known for the notion that in every job there is one best way to proceed (see Taylor, 1967).

"Administrative management theorists" (Fayol, 1949; Gulick and Urwick, 1937) took a broader view of the organization than Taylor, whose primary concern was work efficiency. These theorists were concerned about the major superordinate functions of the total organization such as planning, organizing, staffing, directing, coordinating, reporting, control, and budgeting. They studied these functions within the classic bureaucratic organization, which provided for rules, roles, goals, vertical hierarchy, and division of labor. One of their most important concepts is the distinction between "line" and "staff" personnel. Line personnel are those who actually carry out the specific production tasks of the organization; staff personnel provide support, technical counsel, and resources to both line personnel and top management. This distinction between line and staff is kept in most organizations today and promotes efficiency. However, it also gives rise to two serious complications (Weiner, 1978):

1. Lines of authority can be crossed. For example, a personnel manager (staff) could complain that a service manager (line) had hired a line worker without going through the standard personnel procedure.
2. In order for work to be done, intraorganizational relationships must be developed, since Weber's clear lines of authority are obscured.

A manager must be aware of these complications and must be able to discuss them openly with staff. One's style of leadership in dealing with such problems will be adopted by staff. If the manager is comfortable with the crossing of authority lines and with intraorganization linkages, so will the staff be comfortable, and vice versa.

While all of the foregoing theories and ideas have concentrated on the structure and tasks of the organization, the "human relations movement" concentrates on the social and relationship aspects of the work environment. The now classic Hawthorne studies done by Elton Mayo and his associates in the 1930s (Mayo, 1933; Roethlisberger and Dickson, 1939) at the Hawthorne plant of the Western Electric Company form the cornerstone of this movement. The original studies were designed to determine what influence the physical work environment has on productivity. Although they were not surprised to find that increased productivity is related to improved working conditions, the researchers were indeed surprised that the attention paid to workers has a greater effect on productivity than improvements in the physical aspects of the work environment. These findings caused the researchers to focus on the feelings and attitudes of the workers and on the influence of informal coalitions of workers.

The main ideas of the human relations movement may be summarized as follows:

1. Organizations are social as well as economic and technical entities.
2. The informal work group is crucial to an understanding of organizational behavior. For example, the informal group is an important factor in management succession (as discussed in Chapter 1).
3. Productivity is intimately related to worker satisfaction.
4. Worker motivation is based upon more than just economic considerations. Social-psychological needs must be taken into account.
5. Worker participation is important, especially in terms of communication and decisionmaking.
6. Leadership styles must include *both* democratic *and* authoritarian approaches.

The human relations movement, quite popular since the 1940s and still going strong, has not attempted to replace the "one best way" mentality of earlier schools. While accepting their findings, it attempts benevolently to achieve greater productivity through job satisfaction. Seminars and workshops on group dynamics, promoting positive attitudes, communication skills, and dynamic leadership, are offered to managers in an attempt to help them create a synthesis of the so-called one best way and humanism.

During the 1950s and 1960s researchers from the behavioral sciences began to study organizational life within the framework of the human relations movement and began to challenge the rigidity and singlemindedness of the classical schools of Weber, Taylor, Fayol, and others. Absolutism began to give way to provisionalism or a sort of contingency management (see the discussion of situational leadership in Chapter 3). The notion of contingency was one of many factors that helped spawn open-systems theory.

"Systems theory" is the last organization theory that we will consider. Human services organizations, like many other kinds of organizations, are marked by complicated, divergent, and often conflicting roles, goals and relationships. Systems theory is useful in unraveling the complexities of organizations (Katz and Kahn, 1978). Von Bertalanffy (1968) has described living systems, including social systems, in terms of their relationship with the environment. Essentially, a living system takes in information and resources ("input"), processes them ("throughput"), and exports the transformed inputs ("output") back into the environment, as Figure 2–1 illustrates. The quantity and complexity of inputs are very important to the life of the organization. For example, Aiken and Hage (1968) found that among sixteen human services organizations, those that were highly interdependent (that is, sharing many programs with other organizations) tended to employ a greater variety of professionals, to be more innovative, to have workers who engaged in more professional activities, to have more active internal communication networks, and to be somewhat more decentralized.

A system whose boundaries are so rigid and impermeable that few and homogeneous inputs are allowed will begin to decay and will in turn be less effective in achieving its goals (White, 1978a). In this regard, Schulberg (1975), following Lawrence and Lorsch (1967), suggested that human services organizations need to work hard to promote internal and external linkages for their clients in order to avoid the myopic approach characteristic of specialization and categorical programming. Translated into daily operations this means, for example, that an outpatient therapist in a community mental health center who provides psychotherapy for a school-phobic child but refuses to work with the family or with the child's teachers is not doing what might be necessary to treat the whole problem.

Another important idea from systems theory is that changes in one part of a system will produce changes in other parts of the system. An example of this phenomenon would be the effect of requiring intake workers in a

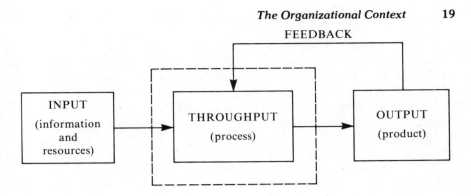

FIGURE 2.1. A simple system.

family service agency to increase intakes by 5 percent. This one change in the intake function would have a ripple effect in those parts of the system responsible for assigning caseworkers, billing clients, monitoring client records, and so on. Each of these systemic changes in turn would set off other changes in the total system. Middle managers must be aware of this property of systems whenever they plan alterations in their programs. They must anticipate and/or control for unwanted side effects and for possible resistance from workers, fellow middle managers, and top management.

Two other aspects of systems theory need to be mentioned here. The first is the notion of "equifinality," which refers to the fact that there is more than one way to produce an outcome in an open system. Equifinality in the open system corresponds to the one best way notion in the closed system. Although there may be one best way to achieve a certain result under certain circumstances, a general principle of open-systems theory is that there may be several methods of producing a particular outcome.

The other aspect of systems theory to be mentioned is "entropy," which refers to the tendency of systems with limited, restricted, or no inputs to run down and lose their differentiated structures. The logical extension of entropy is the death of the system. We are all familiar with the type of organization that is so closed to its external environment that it either shuts down or is subsumed by a more vital, open-system organization.

Systems theory is more than a theory of inputs, throughputs, and outputs, of equifinality and entropy, and of boundaries. This theory also concerns itself, in complicated ways, with how organizations cross their own boundaries to procure varied inputs and subdivide internally to transform inputs to outputs in a manner efficient enough to assure continued support from the environment. The following sections discuss these subdivision and procurement issues.

Although each of the above theories has been described separately, they are not mutually exclusive. The middle manager in the human services will find that a grasp of all these ideas will help one to understand the way things happen in one's organization and, with this understanding, will enable the manager to be an agent of change and improvement in the organization.

Before going on, however, a word must be said about a dynamic tension that is a daily reality for the human services manager. The tension arises between the structural and technical aspects of the organization, on the one hand, and the expectations, values, and beliefs of individual workers, on the other. Organizational goals do not always coincide with individual goals. A threadbare example is the individual whose goal is a higher salary and who works in an organization committed, of necessity, to cost containment. The essence of the manager's daily work is the mediation of these two countervailing forces. As we review formal and informal structures and organizational vitality, this tension will be highlighted.

ORGANIZATIONAL DESIGN

Perlman and Tornatzky (1975) have written, "Building an organization that can address all aspects of the task environment helps to achieve maximum efficiency" (p. 29). The design of the organization is a representation of the internal structure of an organization that shows lines of authority, relationships among the organization's components, and, ideally, something about how the organization's products are generated through the transformation of resources. Ignoring minor variations, the organizational designer has two basic choices of designs to achieve these ends. The first is the traditional "pyramidal design," illustrated in Figure 2-2, with centralized authority at the top and a broad base of line personnel at the bottom. A pyramidal design can be either "goal-oriented" or "process-oriented." Goal-oriented designs are based on a division of the organization according to different products or different client needs. Various divisions in the goal-oriented design may have their own accounting staff, personnel office, legal advisors, and technicians. Each department or division has a high degree of autonomy. Important considerations for a goal-oriented organization are the consumers it serves, the geographical area it serves, and the urgency of the demand for its services or products.

Process-oriented organizations, on the other hand, emphasize resources rather than clients. Specialists are grouped into departments according to the type of work they do instead of according to the type of client they serve. Internal differentiation within a process-oriented organization is by the tasks to be performed and the appropriate technology for each task. This avoids duplication of resources by allowing each functional department to draw upon the special resources of other departments.

The characteristics and goals of the organization will determine whether goal or process orientation is more suitable. Process-oriented forms are

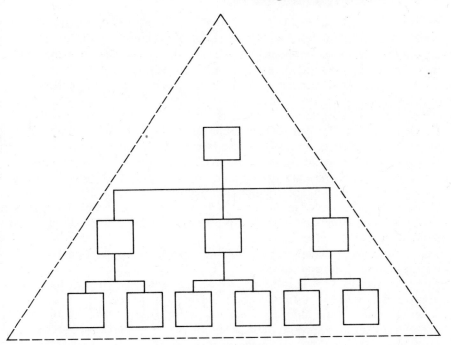

FIGURE 2.2.   Pyramidal organization structure.

more appropriate for organizations that must make maximum use of scarce resources. Where client services are emphasized, the goal-oriented structure is more desirable. But these two orientations, as we shall see, are not mutually exclusive.

Human services organizations have characteristics that make them well suited to *both* orientations. A human services organization's raison d'etre is the special needs of clients, which suggests a goal-oriented structure. Nevertheless, resources in the human services are almost always scarce and must be conserved, a constraint that suggests process orientation. This dilemma leads us to the second choice an organizational designer has in attempting to achieve maximum efficiency by addressing the task environment. The "matrix organization" has been well described by Galbraith (1971, 1973), Wedel (1976), and, in terms of its application to a community mental health center, White (1978b). The matrix design combines goal and process orientation. Individuals who are members of functional (or process) units may also be assigned on either a full- or a part-time basis to goal-oriented projects. Figure 2–3 depicts a simple matrix design, clearly a departure from the classic pyramid. Since workers are permanently assigned to functional departments on the horizontal axis and on an ad hoc basis to special projects on the vertical axis, the matrix allows for a great deal of organizational flexibility. This feature is particularly attractive in human services organizations, which must continually respond to a variety of sometimes conflicting constituencies such as governmental regulatory agencies, citizen boards, funding agencies, and shifting client needs and demands.

The matrix structure has been attracting a great deal of attention over the past few years. This popularity is well deserved, but a caution is in order. Several limitations of the matrix have been described by Davis and Lawrence (1978). The problem deserving particular attention here is dual reporting. A worker in a matrix organization will have two or more bosses. One boss is in charge of the department to which the person is permanently assigned. Other bosses are in charge of the goal-oriented projects on the vertical axis of the table of organization (see Figure 2-3.). All levels of management must be aware of the potential for conflicts of interest and must take special care to clarify rules for reporting. This problem is discussed in detail by White (1978b).

Organizations, whether pyramidal or matrix, have certain common characteristics (Katz and Kahn, 1978). These common characteristics define what the organization *is* in terms of its values, its ways of getting things done, and its leadership. In addition to having a structure, discussed above, an organization must have a formal role pattern—a way of defining who does what. Another necessary characteristic is a clear hierarchy of responsibility and authority. An organization must also have adaptive structures;

FIGURE 2.3.   Matrix organization structure.

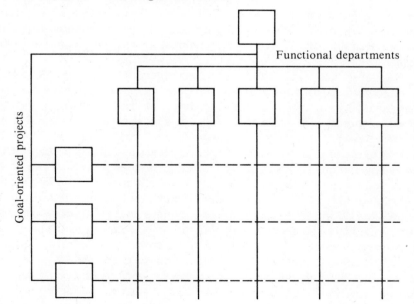

that is, it must have a way to process information that indicates whether or not it is achieving its goals in a manner in keeping with espoused values. Another way of saying this is that it must have "feedback loops." Finally, an organization must have a way of defining why it exists; it must have an ideology. People working in an organization must be continually informed of the nature of that organization's defining characteristics. This is done through formal ways such as written policies, rules and regulations, tables of organization, and statements of purpose. Information about the nature of an organization is also transmitted in informal, even subtle ways that may not be readily apparent to the casual observer.

DOMAIN THEORY

In the introduction to this chapter I alluded to the fact that traditional organizational theory does not adequately explain the unique nature of human services organizations. Nevertheless, most of this chapter has focused on traditional notions of organizations. I took this approach for three reasons. First, traditional organizational theory is useful in describing how work and responsibilities in organizations can be divided and assigned. Second, the traditional approach is the one most commonly used to describe and explain organizations. Finally, there is very little literature that examines the characteristics of human services organizations that are not shared by business and industrial concerns.

The hierarchies and departmentation of the organizational designs that we have discussed so far come to us from business and industry. But what is missing in these designs? The answer is readily apparent when one considers two powerful realms that exist along with the management hierarchy in human services organizations. These two realms are the governing board and the professional staff. Each of the three realms, or, as we shall come to call them, domains of governing board, management, and professional staff has its own value system and mode of operation.

"Domain theory" (Kouzes, Jerrell, Bergthold, Mico, and Vander Plas, 1978; Kouzes and Mico, 1979) has been recently advanced to explain this state of affairs in human services organizations. Different people at different levels of the organization see things differently and therefore organize their work and structure themselves in different ways. They are also guided by different principles and values. Kouzes and co-workers (1978, 1979) have labeled the three domains the "policy domain," the "management domain," and the "service domain." Since the values and other characteristics of each domain differ so dramatically, there is usually discordance, disjunction, and conflict among the three domains. Figure 2–4 depicts each domain with its principles, success measures, structure, and work modes.

POLICY DOMAIN

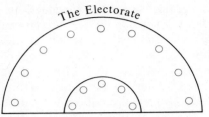

Principles:	Consent of the governed
Success Measures:	Equity
Structure:	Representative Participative
Work Modes:	Voting Bargaining Negotiating

///////////////////////////////////////
/Discordance /Disjunction 'Conflict/
///////////////////////////////////////

MANAGEMENT DOMAIN

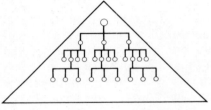

Principles:	Hierarchical control and coordination
Success Measures:	Cost efficiency Effectiveness
Structure:	Bureaucratic
Work Modes:	Linear techniques and tools

///////////////////////////////////////
/Discordance //Disjunction / Conflict //
///////////////////////////////////////.

SERVICE DOMAIN

Principles:	Autonomy Self-regulation
Success Measures:	Quality of service Good standards of practice
Structure:	Collegial
Work Modes:	Client-specific problem-solving

Clients

FIGURE 2.4.   The Three Domains of Human Services Organizations. Reproduced with permission from James M. Kouzes and Paul R. Mico, "Domain Theory: An Introduction to Organizational Behavior in Human Service Organizations." *The Journal of Applied Behavioral Science,* **Vol. 15, No. 4, 1979. Copyright © 1979 by James M. Kouzes and Paul R. Mico.**

The manager's first task regarding the three domains is to be constantly aware that they exist and that their characteristics explain a good deal of the conflict that may arise in a human services organization. Too often managers focus only on the management domain and are puzzled by conflicts among the governing board, the professional staff, and the management domain. Awareness of the three domains gives the manager the language to describe and understand the complexities and vagaries of human services organizations.

This understanding allows the manager to accomplish the second task regarding the three domains: mediating conflict among the domains. This is done by interpreting the values and characteristics of each domain to the members of the other two domains so that dialogue and mutual respect and understanding may develop. The mediation process, complicated by the unique qualities of each domain in each human services organization, involves trade-offs, frustrations, compromises, and showdowns.

Much work remains to be done regarding he implications of domain theory for day-to-day management. However, Kouzes and Mico (1979) suggested that in addition to being aware of the three domains the manager should create opportunities for people in human services organizations to grapple with the many tensions caused by interaction among conflicting domains. In this manner the "demon" is named, becoming real and thus much more amenable to interventions that reduce organizational tension.

THE INFORMAL GROUP

The informal group, mentioned in Chapter 1 and an important finding of the Hawthorne studies, arises in every organization from the interactions of people in ways that are not, indeed cannot be, depicted on the table of organization. Since a great deal of modern management research indicates that effective managers *manage people* whereas ineffective managers *administer organizations* (Wren, 1974), informal groups must be understood and used by the manager. For the present discussion the term "informal groups" will refer to the social networks of employees that are independent of formally defined organizational structure. Katz and Kahn (1978) cogently argued that the term is not precise since an organization may have many undefined dimensions of the formal structure, and all relevant cycles of behavior should be included for study and definition. Nonetheless, for this limited discussion of organizational behavior, the term will be useful.

Productivity and morale are influenced heavily by informal groups, which have several major functions in the organization. One function has to do with social control and conformity. The informal group norms will, for example, dictate how much and what kind of interaction is acceptable for a line worker to have with a superior. Transgressions of these norms are punished by loss of access to two of the other functions of the informal group: the communication network and status.

The communication network, or the grapevine, is one of the most important aspects of the informal group. For example, in one hospital the housekeeping staff, which occupied the lowest level of the formal hierarchy, always knew of impending across-the-board cost-of-living raises before most of the department heads had heard any word on the subject. A network as effective as that can also be the source of rumors, which can be quite destructive in an organization. Managers can control rumors by giving as much accurate information as possible to their subordinates and especially to leaders of the informal group. Secrets coupled with low morale breed rumors. Managers who wish to avoid rumors should also avoid secrets because when more than one person knows something, there is no secret. The best kept secret in most organizations is that secrets are not secret.

Status for members of the informal group is another of its functions and should not be tampered with by managers. Secretaries, housekeepers, nurses' aides, and other line workers, especially those at the lower end of the pay scale, seek status in the informal group to give meaning to an other-wise rather dull existence at work. The hospital housekeepers mentioned above had their day of glory when the pay increase that they had predicted was finally announced. Before the official announcement those "in the know" were much sought after by those who wanted to know the source of the housekeepers' information. Without carrying this point too far, a manager would do well to show respect for the high status members of the various informal groups in the organization and to involve them in discussions of impending decisions or planned changes. These inroads into the informal group, if effective, will pay high dividends in increased worker cooperation later on.

In terms of change, another function of the informal group deserves mention here. As with any social structure, the informal group in an organization will seek to perpetuate itself and its culture. This is usually done by a near religious adherence to the status quo and the belief that what has been good in the past is, and will always be, good. A manager who confronts this belief directly with an unpopular or unexplained change will meet with a degree of overt or covert resistance that may necessitate an embarrassing retreat. Once again, the manager would do well to persuade one or two influential group members of the wisdom of the planned change and avoid frontal attacks.

Informal groups are composed not only of secretaries and housekeepers but of all line and staff workers on all levels of the hierarchy. Human services managers know from experience that higher status professionals can marshall some fairly sophisticated rationalizations to resist the plans of managers. A hospital administrator was given responsibility for the renovation of a "quiet room" in a psychiatric ward. He was approached by a nurse, a psychologist, a social worker, and three psychiatrists who told him that the color he had picked for the walls would be too stimulating to agitated patients. Each of these well-trained and well-respected professionals suggested a different color as the most soothing and therapeutic! Another variation on this theme is resistance to planned change based on the tired argument that "the change you propose will be detrimental to service delivery; our clients will suffer." This is, as you know, not necessarily so.

The goals, interests, and methods of the formal organization and the informal group must be integrated. In order to do this the manager should spend time with line and staff personnel to let them know that their ideas and attitudes are considered important. Decisionmaking committees should have representatives from all levels of the formal organization. Finally, the manager should not make any promises to workers without being sure they can be kept. Placating staff with false promises is sometimes tempting and useful in the short run, but the promises almost always come back to haunt the manager at a later time.

ORGANIZATIONAL VITALITY

In the earlier discussion of systems theory the importance of a variety of inputs was briefly mentioned as a determinant of organizational vitality. This chapter will end with a short discussion of a few other conditions of a lively and energetic organization over which middle managers may exert some influence. To begin, an organization must have the capacity for self-criticism: it must be able to examine itself to determine, in a rational manner, whether or not particular courses of action are appropriate means of achieving its goals within the value structure of the organization.

An extension of this idea is that a lively organization must have a fluidity of structure such that obsolete departments can be phased out, modified, or merged with other departments. Similarly, obsolete procedures must be easily and quickly changed or dropped. As important as change is, though, the strong, vital organization must have the ability to stabilize its structures and procedures so that its members can get on with its real work. Communication of changes and the ease with which communication flows downward and, especially, upward in the formal organization are also essential to the organization. This issue will be discussed more fully in a subsequent chapter.

One of the most important resources in an energetic organization is people. An organization must be able to attract bright, spirited, and motivated people at all levels. New people bring new ideas and new ways of doing things and are therefore a hedge against stagnation and entropy. On the other hand, the organization must allow for its veterans to move on to new jobs in which they can continue to grow. Human services organizations tend to be very warm, nurturing places for staff members. Such an environment can be what many young, inexperienced human services workers need to learn and develop skills, gain confidence, and determine the direction their careers will take. After a couple of years, though, these young people, who lack experience in other settings, may become bored with their work. Some of them, because of the nurturing atmosphere they are working in, are hesitant to meet new challenges. These are the people who may become the staunchest defenders of the status quo in an organization and prove quite destructive of its vitality. They also can be quite destructive to themselves because of the many conflicts that a failure to leave the nest can engender. The middle manager will do well by the organization *and* the occasional stuck worker to encourage him or her to move on to new opportunities for professional growth and development. The manager, however, must approach this unpleasant task cautiously lest he be misunderstood and accused of running off the best and most experienced people.

Another task of the middle manager who seeks to preserve organizational vitality is to combat vested interests of subgroups that may subvert the goals of the entire organization. In any organization there are factions that hold points of view and opinions that may not be in keeping with the total organization's values and goals. Also, the people who do one specific task in an organization, such as determine the eligibility of clients for services, may compete with others in the organization, such as service providers, for resources, recognition, higher pay, and special privileges. The manager must insure that all parts of the organization are allowed to maintain their individual identities and status. He must also, paradoxically, integrate the parts of the structure into an effective whole that seeks to achieve the goals of the entire organization. The effort to coordinate and link the work of individuals and groups is a continuous maintenance function of management.

The effective middle manager should keep staff focused on the goals of the organization and on its future. To focus on the past in a way that makes old ways of doing things and past leaders inordinately attractive can be very painful for an organization and can, if continued, threaten its very existence. In this regard, high motivation and morale are essential. The middle manager must continually strive to see that all subordinates share a conviction that what they are doing is useful and important.

REFERENCES

AIKEN, M., AND HAGE, J. "Organizational interdependence and intraorganizational structure." *American Sociological Review* (1968) 33(2):219.

DAVIS, S. M., AND LAWRENCE, P. R. "Problems of matrix organizations." *Harvard Business Review* (1978) 56(3):131–142.

FAYOL, H. *General and Industrial Management*. Translated by C. Storrs. London: Pitman, 1949.

GALBRAITH, J. R. "Matrix organization designs." *Business Horizons* (1971) 14(1):29–40.

_____. *Designing Complex Organizations*. Reading: Addison-Wesley, 1973.

GULICK, L., AND URWICK, L. (eds.). *Papers on the Science of Administration*. New York: Institute of Public Administration, 1937.

KATZ, D., AND KAHN, R. L. *The Social Psychology of Organizations*. 2d edition. New York: Wiley, 1978.

KOUZES, J. M., JERRELL, J. M., BERGTHOLD, G. D., MICO, P. R., AND VANDER PLAS, G. P. *Developing Effective Mental Health Organizations*. San Jose: Joint Center for Human Services Development, San Jose State University, 1978.

KOUZES, J. M., AND MICO, P. R. "Domain theory: an introduction to organizational behavior in human service organizations." *Journal of Applied Behavioral Science* (1979) 45(4):449–469.

LAWRENCE, P. R., AND LORSCH, J. W. *Organization and Environment*. Boston: Division of Research, Harvard Business School, 1967.

MAYO, E. *The Human Problems of an Industrial Civilization*. Boston: Harvard Business School, 1933.

PERLMAN, B., AND TORNATZKY, L. G. "Organizational perspective on community mental health centers." *Administration in Mental Health* (1975) 3(1):27–31.

ROETHLISBERGER, F. J., AND DICKSON, W. J. *Management and the Worker*. Cambridge: Harvard University Press, 1939.

SCHULBERG, H. C. "Administrative structures and human services for children." *Administration in Mental Health* (1975) 3(1):32–42.

TAYLOR, F. W. *The Principles of Scientific Management*. New York: Norton, 1967.

VON BERTALANFFY, L. *General Systems Theory*. New York: Braziller, 1968.

WEBER, M. *The Theory of Social and Economic Organization*. Translated by A. M. Henderson and T. Parsons. New York: Free Press, 1964.

WEDEL, K. R. "Matrix design for human service organizations." *Administration in Mental Health* (1976) 4(1):36–42.

WEINER, M. E. "Application of organizational and systems theory to human services reform." *Human Services Monograph Series*, number 6. Washington, D.C.: Project Share, April 1978.

WHITE, S. L. "Family theory according to the Cambridge model." *Journal of Marriage and Family Counseling* (1978a) 4(2):91–100.

_____. "The community mental health center as a matrix organization." *Administration in Mental Health* (1978b) 6(2):99–106.

WREN, G. P. *Modern Health Administration*. Athens: University of Georgia Press, 1974.

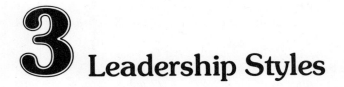

3 Leadership Styles

Leadership and management are terms that are often used to mean the same thing. In this book, I shall use the term "leadership" to denote the behaviors that managers use to influence other people to work toward organizational goals. Leaders inspire others to follow them for the sake of the organization. Not all managers are leaders, just as all leaders in an organization are not necessarily managers. Leadership, however, is a skill without which a manager's job will always be more difficult and at times quite impossible. Without leaders, both formal and informal, the members of the organization will not come together into a unified group working toward objectives that supersede individual goals.

In this chapter we shall examine a few of the more important research efforts in leadership. The characteristics of good leadership and the ways that they can be acquired and applied will be discussed. And we shall pay special attention to situational or contingency leadership, which takes into account the personal characteristics of the leader, the task to be accomplished, and the motivation of the followers. For the purposes of this chapter the terms "situational" and "contingency" will be used interchangeably when referring to leadership. Hollander (1978) suggested that the situational approach to leadership has too narrow a focus and does not consider the complexity of the leader-follower transactional field as does the contingency approach. However, the beginning manager will find these terms, which will be defined and discussed shortly, too close in meaning to be concerned about Hollander's thoughtful distinction.

APPROACHES TO LEADERSHIP

Over the years there have been many notions about how a manager can become a good leader. A manager is a *head* of a work group because he is the officially designated leader of the group. Brown (1965) pointed out that an "official leader is often called the *head* in social psychology to distinguish him from an informal leader. The head of a group is likely to be disproportionately influential but he is not invariably so; *headship* can be rejected" (p. 679). Later in this chapter we shall examine the question of whether leaders are born or made. For now, however, we shall confine our attention to some of the ways social psychologists and managers have viewed leadership in management.

The scientific management school, with its emphasis on efficient production, advocated a rather hard-nosed approach to leadership. The effective leader was someone who could produce the most in the shortest period of time with the least amount of resources. Little or no thought was given to the effect this approach would have on those who were expected to do the work—"If they aren't happy here, they can leave. Everyone is expendable."

Managers began to pay attention to the feelings and attitudes of workers as the human relations movement was popularized in the management literature from the 1930s through the early 1950s. The basic idea of the movement, as we saw in the previous chapter, is that the effective leader has a sincere interest in his subordinates as people, recognizes the importance of the informal group, is concerned about the job satisfaction of workers, recognizes the psychosocial needs of workers, involves workers as much as possible in decisions that affect them, and does not relate to workers as though they were machines.

Steinmetz and Todd (1975) pointed out three major problems with the human relations movement. First, many managers are simply not good at human relations. Those people who are most likely to be managers often are those people with a need to make a name for themselves through high production. When this kind of manager tries to use a human relations approach his attempts can come off as stiff and something less than genuine.

A second problem with the human relations movement is that some managers try to buy happiness in their organizations. They do this by offering extras to *all* workers regardless of performance, an approach based on a simplistic interpretation of the Hawthorne studies; namely, happy employees are productive employees. Experience with what has been termed "country club management" has indicated that the problem of effective leadership and productivity is more complicated than the happiness of workers.

The third problem with the human relations movement as described by Steinmetz and Todd is a special problem for many human services managers with a background in certain schools of psychology. That is, some people resent being "psyched out" or showered with concern and warm feelings. Some people are by nature private people who would rather not have others prying into their personal lives even with seemingly innocuous displays of politeness and concern. Similarly, those who wish to lead (and be followed) would do well to avoid the presumptuous practice of describing the behavior of errant workers in such clinical terms as "passive-aggressive," "paranoid," "sociopathic," and, one that is often applied to women, "hysterical."

Two more abuses should be added to Steinmetz and Todd's list of problems with the human relations movement. In the eagerness of some managers to look after the morale and professional development of subordinates, concern for the goals of the organization sometimes gets lost. Weissman (1973) charged that many human services organizations operate more in the interest of their employees than in the interest of their clients. Concern for employees must be balanced with concern for productivity and organizational goals.

Finally, neither the scientific management school nor the human relations movement takes into account the complexity of the leader-task-follower field. Some combinations of workers and tasks call for certain leadership styles while other worker-task combinations call for other leadership styles. This correspondence is complicated by the personality and attitudes of the manager and the ways he interacts with various worker-task combinations. Let us turn our attention now to the role of followership in determining leadership styles.

FOLLOWING THE LEADER

A discussion of leadership that does not consider followers is incomplete (Burns, 1978; Hollander, 1978). A modern systems view of interpersonal behavior impels us to take the leader's entire social field into account. This field includes those who follow the leader since simple logic shows us that there can be no leading if there is no one to follow. Studies of the family have shown that families that produce profoundly disturbed offspring are often marked by a pattern of communication dominated by disqualification (Haley, 1959). Such families are unable to maintain stable coalitions partly because those who initiate action are not supported or followed by other family members. Organizations cannot function if workers will not or cannot support the initiatives of their managers. Both Hollander and Burns have characterized leadership as a social transaction in which the leader and the follower engage in a give-and-take. Putting it simply, the follower performs a task in return for recognition by the leader, who is in turn gratified by the completion of the task.

The notion that followers must support leaders in order for action to take place is important. Followers have real power by virtue of their ability to empower others by granting them support (Kantor and Lehr, 1975). It is clear, then, that followers may be able to influence the actions of potential leaders by their relative ability or willingness to support the leader by following him. The recognition of the significance of followership can be seen in two major management theories.

The first has to do with the leader's *attitudes* about those people he wishes to follow him. McGregor's (1960) "Theory X" and "Theory Y" suggest two different ways of thinking about followers. Theory X says that people are inherently lazy and unwilling to work; they must be watched over and prodded. Furthermore, it says that most people are not creative and are inept at solving problems. On the other hand, Theory Y states that most people actually like to work if conditions are favorable. It also states that people can be creative and self-directed if they are motivated through increased self-esteem and social benefits and that problem-solving abilities are widely distributed in the population.

McGregor asserted that workers will respond to the expectations leaders have of them. Stated simply, workers will follow managers who subscribe to Theory Y more readily than they will follow managers who subscribe to Theory X. This dynamic interchange between the expectations of managers and workers' perceptions about those expectations are powerful determinants of whether or not leadership through followership will take place in an organization.

Theory Y management became quite popular soon after it was introduced in the early 1960s. It was particularly attractive to managers in the human services because of its humanistic orientation. However, managers quickly found that while the idea seemed to be a good one, it was difficult to put into practice. Steinmetz and Todd (1975) pointed out that supervisors who practiced Theory Y management found, much to their chagrin, that some workers did their work too slowly, or inaccurately, or not at all. This led some researchers to consider more than just managers' attitudes about followers.

The second way in which followership is related to leadership has to do with a manager's *assessment* of the ability and willingness of certain workers to do certain jobs at certain times. This idea of assessing the potential of workers is a part of "situational management," or "contingency management." While Theory Y was another in a long series of attempts to find the single best style of leadership, recent research has shown this search to be futile (Fiedler, 1967; Hersey and Blanchard, 1977). The most effective leaders are those who can continually adapt their behavior to suit the unique demands of the workers and the situation at hand in the ever changing environment of managing work groups. One of the best recent treatments of transactions between leaders and followers is Burns (1978).

SITUATIONAL LEADERSHIP

Hersey and Blanchard's (1977) research-based and eminently practical theory of leadership is predicated on the idea that leaders must be able to regulate the amount of task behavior (goal-oriented direction) and relationship behavior (emotional and social support) they adopt given the level of maturity of the followers and the idiosyncrasies of the situation.

"Task behavior" is a style of leadership characterized by one-way communication from the leader to the workers. The leader explains how and when things should be done and what each worker must do. He also lets each worker know exactly what is expected and asks him to follow a set of standard operating procedures.

At the other end of the spectrum is "relationship behavior," which is characterized by two-way communication between leader and workers. The two-way communication is marked by emotional and social support, facilitating behaviors, and what the transactional analysis people call "strokes." The leader is friendly and approachable and finds time to talk with and listen to workers. He is also flexible and willing to consider changes.

Although we all may be able to think of people who fit one or the other of these behavior types to the letter, Hersey and Blanchard (1977) and Stogdill and Coons (1957) found that these styles manifest themselves in different managers in different ways. Some managers do indeed display more of one style than the other. Most, however, behave in ways characteristic of both styles. These researchers determined that these two polar opposite styles are not dichotomous in the real world of daily management. Figure 3-1 shows how task behavior and relationship behavior can be plotted on two separate axes. The numbers in each box will be used later as an abbreviated way of referring to each leadership style. For example, S2 (style 2) will refer to a leadership style marked by high task and high relationship behavior.

Another dimension of Hersey and Blanchard's theory of leadership is the maturity level of the members in a work group. Maturity is operationally defined by Hersey and Blanchard (1977) as "the capacity to set high but attainable goals (achievement-motivated), willingness and ability to take responsibility, and education and/or experience of an individual or a group. *These variables of maturity should be considered only in relation to a specific task to be performed*" (p. 161). This last point is important because certain workers may display a high level of maturity where one task or project is concerned and a low level of maturity where other tasks are concerned. Consequently, managers must be astute in determining or, more accurately, diagnosing the maturity level of each worker in a work group in relation to each job he must do.

Finally, a manager must be able to diagnose the task environment. That is, he must be able to determine the resources and time available to him and

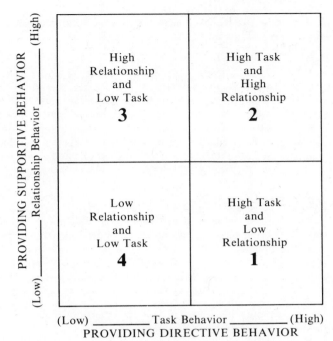

FIGURE 3.1. Four basic leader behavior styles. Reproduced with permission from Paul Hersey and Kenneth H. Blanchard, *Situational Leadership*. Escondido, Calif.: The Center for Leadership Studies, 1976. Copyright © 1976 by Paul Hersey and Kenneth H. Blanchard.

his subordinates to do the job. Additionally, a manager must be prepared to make use of the perceptions of others in determining whether or not his style of leadership in a given situation is effective or ineffective (see Table 3–1).

PUTTING THE THEORY TO WORK

How does the working middle manager make use of this theory? The first step is obvious but must be stated. The task or goal must be determined. That is, the manager must ask himself, "What is it that we want to do?" Second, the manager must determine the maturity level of the work group in relation to the goal. Are the workers able to set high but attainable goals? Are they willing and able to assume responsibility? Are the members of the work group able by training and/or experience to accomplish the task?

TABLE 3-1. How the Basic Leader Behavior Styles May Be Seen by Others When They Are Effective or Ineffective

Basic Styles	Effective	Ineffective
High Task and Low Relationship	Seen as having well-defined methods for accomplishing goals that are helpful to the followers.	Seen as imposing methods on others; sometimes seen as unpleasant, and interested only in short-run output.
High Task and High Relationship	Seen as satisfying the needs of the group for setting goals and organizing work, but also providing high levels of socioemotional support.	Seen as initiating more structure than is needed by the group and often appears not to be genuine in interpersonal relationships.
High Relationship and Low Task	Seen as having implicit trust in people and as being primarily concerned with facilitating their goal accomplishment.	Seen as primarily interested in harmony; sometimes seen as unwilling to accomplish a task if it risks disrupting a relationship or losing "good person" image.
Low Relationship and Low Task	Seen as appropriately delegating to subordinates decisions about how the work should be done and providing little socioemotional support where little is needed by the group.	Seen as providing little structure or socioemotional support when needed by members of the group.

From *Management of Organizational Behavior*, 3rd edition, by Paul Hersey and Kenneth M. Blanchard, © 1977, Prentice-Hall, Inc. and adapted from *Managerial Effectiveness* by W. J. Reddin, © 1970, McGraw-Hill Book Company. Reprinted by permission of Prentice-Hall, Inc. and McGraw-Hill Book Company.

After answering these questions, the manager determines whether the group has a high maturity level (M4), a moderate level of maturity (M3 or M2), or a low maturity level (M1).

Using Figure 3–2, the manager next relates the diagnosed level of maturity (M) to the appropriate leadership style (S). Each leadership style is characterized by a specific behavior, summed up in a key word:

M4 = S4 = DELEGATING = low relationship/low task
M3 = S3 = PARTICIPATING = high relationship/low task
M2 = S2 = SELLING = high task/high relationship
M1 = S1 = TELLING = high task/low relationship

No manager, of course, would take the time to plot worker maturity level and the corresponding leadership style on a graph each time a job needs to be done. This graphic description of situational leadership merely serves as a way of organizing one's thinking in a deliberate manner each time a new task is encountered.

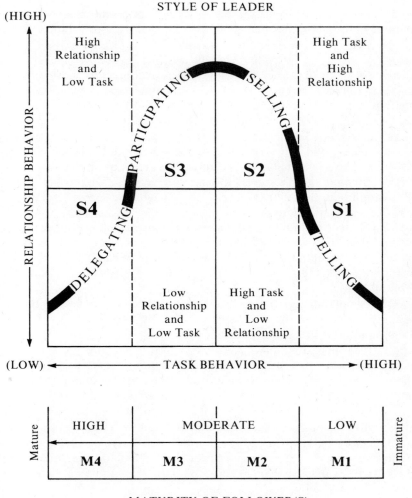

FIGURE 3.2. Situational Leadership. Reproduced with permission from Paul Hersey and Kenneth H. Blanchard, *Situational Leadership*. Escondido, Calif.: The Center for Leadership Studies, 1976. Copyright © 1976 by Paul Hersey and Kenneth H. Blanchard.

INCREASING LEVELS OF MATURITY

Hersey and Blanchard have made provisions in their theory for helping workers increase their level of maturity through behavior modification. Workers with a low level of maturity must be approached by their manager with high task and low relationship behavior. As the maturity of the workers increases, the manager can increase relationship behavior and decrease task behavior. The change in the manager's approach must be slow and gradual so that workers do not exploit the high relationship and low task stance by lowering productivity. That is, sudden shifts in the manager's behavior in terms of the degree of task versus relationship can promote confusion and ill will among workers. Workers may respond by lowering productivity after the manager exhibits low task and high relationship behavior. Gradual changes in manager behavior will be more readily understood as responses to worker behavior whereas abrupt changes could be perceived as inconsistent and unwarranted. On the other hand, the manager who wishes to increase the maturity level of workers must begin to allow workers to take more and more responsibility for their work. If the workers are able to maintain high productivity levels the manager can increase relationship behavior and continue to decrease task behavior: "This is a two step process: first, reduction in direction, and *if adequate performance follows*; second, increase in socioemotional support as reinforcement. This process should continue until the follower is assuming significant responsibility and performing as an individual of moderate maturity" (Hersey and Blanchard, 1976, pp. 3–4).

The idea of helping followers to increase their maturity level in the manner outlined above is firmly rooted in work by Likert (1961), Livingston (1969), and others that indicates that people respond positively to the high expectations their superiors have of them. Moreover, people tend to perform poorly when their managers implicitly expect them to perform poorly. The human services manager should take heed of this important tenet of modern management. It is, however, also important for the human services manager not to expect the professional to produce work at superhuman levels. This possibility is a real danger in agencies with waiting lists for services and in agencies funded through purchase of service agreements with funding sources. The desire to serve needy clients and to assure high revenue levels can force the manager to expect too much from underpaid professionals. The human services middle manager is nearly always in the precarious position of being responsible for his program's producing too little by expecting too little or, ironically, too much from subordinates.

We have spent a great deal of time examining different types of leadership styles as they relate to the varying types of potential followers. It is also important to note that leadership style will vary according to the characteristics of the organization in which leader-follower transactions occur (for more on this subject see Etzioni, 1964).

THE MAKING OF A LEADER

Theodore White, the author of *The Making of the President* series, argued in *In Search of History* (1978) that history is shaped by great men who know how to seize and hold power. Parenthetically, he noted that Mao Tse-tung and Chou En-lai were victorious over Chiang Kai-shek largely because the Communists were able to give aid and succor to the populace while fighting the Japanese whereas the Nationalists under Chiang were not perceived as advocates of anyone but themselves. White's thesis echoes what is called the "great man" leadership theory that leaders are born, not made (Hollander, 1978). As we take a casual look at the great leaders of history, this notion has its appeal. We all would certainly like to have even half the charisma of such great leaders as Winston Churchill or John F. Kennedy. We would also like to possess some of the characteristics mentioned by those who espouse the "trait approach" to leadership: courage, wisdom, character, genius. While intelligence and courage are important in becoming a leader, the situational approach described earlier and the transactional approach described by Hollander can be adopted by the professional willing to make sufficient effort. Leaders can be made, given intelligence, effort, and opportunity.

In addition, a professional who wishes to lead must remember a few other things. He must remember the goals of the organization in a manner bordering on singlemindedness. Although these goals are often forgotten in the turbulence that marks so many human services agencies, goals give the organization meaning and structure. The aspiring leader must be willing to be tough and task-oriented when necessary. Also he must be willing and able to be personable when appropriate. But above all, the professional who wishes to be a leader must be honest. The temptation to be dishonest is everywhere in an organization. Sometimes this temptation takes quite a benevolent form; for example, it is easier to tell an employee who is being fired that he is being let go because of funding cutbacks instead of telling him the real reasons, reasons that may be unpleasant to discuss and painful for the employee to hear. At times managers are tempted to justify dishonest actions or statements by saying that the good of the organization is at stake. That kind of rationalization may have some short-term benefits but will probably compromise the manager's integrity and will severely compromise his ability to lead.

The ability to be flexible and sensitive to one's workers are qualities that are implied in situational leadership. Other qualities of a good leader are also important. Leaders will not be followed if they do not command the respect and confidence of their subordinates. Conversely, the leader must show respect for and confidence in his subordinates. The leader must be able to demonstrate that he is competent in his department's specialty area and, equally important, that he is competent to make management decisions that will profoundly affect the work environment. Loyalty is another key quality of a good leader; he must be loyal not only to the organization and its goals but also to his subordinates. A good leader must be dependable and available to his subordinates. He must always be around to answer questions and to allay anxiety and uncertainty in subordinates. In order to answer subordinates' questions in a way that will enable them to continue to work toward the organization's goals, the leader must be a thoughtful person who exercises good judgment. He must not be so thoughtful, however, that he cannot be decisive, for indecisiveness causes followers to flounder. Finally, a good leader must be sociable and must radiate a certain amount of enthusiasm for the work that the organization is about.

We shall now turn our attention to specific skills necessary in managerial work and specific tasks that require effective leaders with management, as well as technical or clinical, skills.

REFERENCES

BROWN, R. *Social Psychology*. New York: Free Press, 1965.

BURNS, J. M. *Leadership*. New York: Harper & Row, 1978.

ETZIONI, A. *Modern Organizations*. Englewood Cliffs: Prentice-Hall, 1964.

FIEDLER, F. E. *A Theory of Leadership Effectiveness*. New York: McGraw-Hill, 1967.

GREINER, L. E. "Evolution and revolution as organizations grow." *Harvard Business Review* (1972) 50(4):37–46.

HALEY, J. "The family of the schizophrenic: a model system." *Journal of Nervous and Mental Disease* (1959) 129(4):357–374.

HERSEY, P., AND BLANCHARD, K. H. *Situational Leadership*. San Diego: Center for Leadership Studies, 1976.

———. *Management of Organizational Behavior*. 3d edition. Englewood Cliffs: Prentice-Hall, 1977.

HOLLANDER, E. P. *Leadership Dynamics*. New York: Free Press, 1978.

KANTOR, D., AND LEHR, W. *Inside the Family*. San Francisco: Jossey-Bass, 1975.

LIKERT, R. *New Patterns of Management*. New York: McGraw-Hill, 1961.

LIPPITT, G. L., AND SCHMIDT, W. H. "Crises in a developing organization." *Harvard Business Review* (1967) 45(6):102–112.

LIVINGSTON, J. S. "Pygmalion in management." *Harvard Business Review* (1969) 47(4):81–89.

MCGREGOR, D. *The Human Side of Enterprise*. New York: McGraw-Hill, 1960.

REDDIN, W. J. *Managerial Effectiveness*. New York: McGraw-Hill, 1970.

STEINMETZ, L. L., AND TODD, H. R. *First-line Management*. Dallas: Business Publications, 1975.

STOGDILL, R. M., AND COONS, A. E. (eds.). *Leader Behavior: Its Description and Measurement*. Research Monograph no. 88. Columbus: Bureau of Business Research, Ohio State University, 1957.

WEISSMAN, H. H. *Overcoming Mismanagement in the Human Service Professions*. San Francisco: Jossey-Bass, 1973.

WHITE, T. H. *In Search of History*. New York: Harper & Row, 1978.

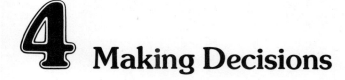

4 Making Decisions

"We have been educated to make distinctions, but not to make decisions," wrote Gail Thain Parker in September 1976. The former president of Bennington College, in an essay on higher education in America, succinctly expressed the dilemma of many clinical managers who are trained as clinicians to make diagnoses and to distinguish between thoughts and feelings, fantasy and reality, eligibility and noneligibility for services. Of course, as Levinson and Klerman (1967) suggested, a clinician must also be able to take decisive action at the appropriate time. But decisionmaking is a task of primary importance among managers, whereas it is, perhaps, of secondary importance among service providers. The decisions made by managers very often affect the workings of an entire organization of people in ways that may have a lasting impact on the work and personal lives of many people. The business of *choosing* is a primary occupation of managers. In this chapter we shall examine managerial decisionmaking, the task of making choices, from a perspective of utility and action.

Just how central is decisionmaking to management? Shull, Delbecq, and Cummings (1970), in discussing the role of managerial decisionmaking in an organizational context, noted that an organization is a self-regulating system attempting to achieve espoused goals, with management functioning as the regulator. The Nobel laureate Herbert Simon (1976) observed that management requires rational decisions, which are defined as the reduction of uncertainty. But it is Mintzberg (1973) who best expressed the centrality of decisionmaking to management. In his study of what administrators actually do with their time, Mintzberg delineated ten "working roles" divided into three groups. One of the groups consists of four "decisional roles": entrepreneur, disturbance handler, resource allocator, and negotiator; we shall examine each role in turn (see Table 4–1).

TABLE 4-1. **Summary of Decisional Roles**

Role	Description	Identifiable Activities
Entrepreneur	Searches organization and its environment for opportunities and initiates "improvement projects" to bring about change; supervises design of certain projects as well	Strategy and review sessions involving initiation or design of improvement projects
Disturbance Handler	Responsible for corrective action when organization faces important, unexpected disturbances	Strategy and review sessions involving disturbances and crises
Resource Allocator	Responsible for the allocation of organizational resources of all kinds—in effect the making or approval of all significant organizational decisions	Scheduling; request for authorization; any activity involving budgeting and the programming of subordinates' work
Negotiator	Responsible for representing the organization at major negotiations	Negotiation

From Table 2, "Decisional Roles," in *The Nature of Managerial Work* by Henry Mintzberg, © 1973 by H. Mintzberg. Reprinted by permission of Harper & Row Publishers, Inc.

The "entrepreneur" is proactive; that is, he initiates action in the organization through innovation. He designs projects and generates ideas. In so doing, the manager must be mindful of the organization's goals and, indeed, must even decide what those goals will be. He searches the organization's environment in order to anticipate problems and opportunities. When problems or opportunities have been identified the manager must decide whether or not the organization will take action to seize the opportunity or remedy the problem. He may, once a decision to act has been made, either delegate the responsibility for action to others or supervise the action himself.

At the other end of the proactive-reactive spectrum is the "disturbance handler," who deals with situations that are not predictable and controllable ahead of time. Unforeseen events, long-neglected problems that come to a head, and conflicts among subordinates are circumstances to which the manager must react in a decisive way. Other disturbances can emerge between the manager's organization and another organization or between subsystems within the organization. These problems occur suddenly and are rarely discovered in the routine flow of organizational information. The manager, who may have more influence and power during times of crisis than at other times, must allow the handling of the disturbance to take priority over other matters. Mintzberg takes issue with the popular belief that crises are a sign of bad management by saying that in the life of any organization even good managers cannot anticipate all eventualities.

In the third decisional role, that of "resource allocator," the manager makes decisions regarding how his own work should be scheduled, how the work of others should be programmed, and whether or not certain actions will be authorized. One of the ways in which actions are authorized is through budgeting—the assignment of specific resources to specific projects. Budget decisions are usually made one or at most two times a year. On a more routine basis, a manager must decide how to allocate resources within the budget. Also, decisions about how to allocate human resources for projects must be made.

The manager's fourth decisional role, according to Mintzberg, is "negotiator." In this role the manager acts as the figurehead or spokesperson for the organization vis-à-vis other agencies. An example of this role that is emerging in the human services is "grant brokering," whereby the manager of one human services organization or subsystem coordinates the design, writing, and implementation of a grant for a project shared with other human services organizations. The negotiator must be able to work out an arrangement that is in keeping with the goals of the project in question. The arrangement must benefit not only one's own organization but also the other agencies involved.

Mintzberg's decisional roles are easily recognized as an important part of the work of anyone who has managed an organization of any size. The remainder of this chapter will take a closer look at five specific areas: the environment in which decisions are made, theories of decisionmaking, the criteria for good decisions, the actual process of making decisions, and how to implement choices.

THE DECISIONMAKING ENVIRONMENT

Before a manager can make any decision he must have a clear sense of the possibilities and limitations of actions. As with so many other facets of management and organizational life, decisions are made within a complicated context that defines what action can be taken and who can take it. Drucker (1977) suggested that a central function of an organization is to answer the question of who has the authority to change the organization. Taking another perspective on the environment of decisionmaking, Thomson and Tuden (1959) pointed out that the kind of decision that gets made depends upon whether there is agreement on objectives and whether goals are clearly stated. But perhaps the most important aspect of the decisionmaking environment is what Shull, Delbecq, and Cummings (1970) called "bounded discretion" and Kaufman (1967) labeled "preformed decisions." The notion that some things cannot be decided upon by some people is crucial in organizations, especially in the kind of bureaucracies that characterize so many human services organizations.

For cooperation to occur in an organization, there must be a set of formal and informal rules, regulations, and policies that specify the limits of individual behavior in certain circumstances. Figure 4–1 shows the levels of constraints on an individual manager's action. At the lower level one has an area of discretion within which one is relatively free to act. As a manager ascends the scale of bounded discretion one is less and less free to exercise a wide range of choices. The most effective managers in human services or-

FIGURE 4.1. Bounded discretion scale. After F. A. Shull, A. L. Delbecq, and L. L. Cummings, *Organizational Decision Making*. New York: McGraw-Hill, 1970.

| Legal restrictions |
| Moral and ethical norms |
| Formal policies and rules |
| Unofficial social norms |
| Discretionary area (acceptable choices for action) |

ganizations are those who can exploit their discretionary boundaries to the fullest. Furthermore, they know when it might be wise to be courageous and cross boundaries and when it is prudent not to do so.

Managers tend to want to make decisions that affect *only* their spheres of influence and are unlikely to acknowledge their responsibility in the larger organization (Lavoie, 1978). Moreover, many managers define their spheres of influence too narrowly. This conservative tendency can be a trap for managers. If a manager's decisions are overly restricted, delayed, or checked out with the boss, he will not be of much use to the boss and will not be an effective advocate for his staff and his program.

Kennedy White House staffer Theodore Sorensen (1963) has given us another view of bounded discretion. He pointed out that the value judgments of decisionmakers are powerful determinants of what gets decided. He added that decisionmakers are free to choose within five limits: (1) permissibility; (2) available resources; (3) available time; (4) previous commitments; and (5) available information. Then he added, "The essence of decision is choice; and, to choose, it is first necessary to know" (p. 39). The problem of the limitations of information and knowledge leads us now to consider three theoretical models for decisionmaking.

THREE DECISIONMAKING MODELS

Exactly how should a clinical manager approach decisionmaking? How should he search for alternatives, consider the merits of each, and, finally, choose the best one? Before considering the answers to these questions it may be useful to consider Townsend's distinction between two general types of decisions. In his popular book *Up the Organization* (1970), he suggested that there are decisions (1) that are difficult to change, such as launching a new project, and (2) those that are not, such as assigning a routine task within the organization. Implicit in this distinction is the notion that some decisions are simple and require uncomplicated research and deliberation. Other decisions have more serious and lasting consequences that cause the decisionmaker to feel more anxiety and give the matter a great deal of time and effort. This is not to suggest that mundane decisions are unimportant. The manager who cannot handle routine decisions quickly and effectively will probably have a great deal of trouble with the big decisions and will probably leave subordinates feeling leaderless and confused. Nevertheless, managers can learn much about little decisions from the ways in which big ones are made. We shall now examine three models of decisionmaking that have been widely described in the management and psychological literature.

The first model is really just that, a model. "Pure rationality" (Dror, 1967), or what Janis and Mann (1977) called "optimizing" is rarely employed in the real world of management decisionmaking. According to this approach, decisionmaking is a series of logical, ordered steps. The goals of the organization are assigned priorities and all the alternatives for action are identified. The alternative with the highest payoff and the least cost is finally chosen. The decisionmaker must examine every conceivable option for action and must estimate the benefits and costs of each. Such careful deliberations assume the availability of unlimited information and unlimited time and money to allow for a careful study of the information. This view also assumes that the human mind can process all available information efficiently and accurately. Janis and Mann (1977) noted that many behavioral scientists regard pure rationality as an ideal method toward which decisionmakers should strive. They also observed that most writers in the field disagree with them over the assumptions made in this model.

"Incrementalism," or "muddling through" is practically the opposite of pure rationality. Lindblom (1959), who coined the term "muddling through," and Wildavsky (1974), who views this model as endemic to the public budgeting process because of the politics involved in that process, are critics of pure rationality and advocate incrementalism. Decisionmaking, according to this view, is a series of moves and countermoves involving both a clash of information and conflicts of interest. Decisionmaking is seen as an essentially political process in that what is important is one's ability to influence others; relevant information is of far less importance than it is in the pure rationality model. Janis and Mann (1977) correctly pointed out that decisionmakers using this model "have no real awareness of trying to arrive at a new policy; rather, there is a never-ending series of attacks on each new problem as it arises" (p. 33). Ultimately, the incremental decisions commit the organization to a course of action not intended and, indeed, not even considered when the first in a series of decisions was made. An excellent, though unpleasant, example of the possible effects of incrementalism over a long period of time is America's involvement in Vietnam from the Truman years through the Johnson years (Halberstam, 1972).

By now it is clear that neither pure rationality nor incrementalism is an acceptable model of decisionmaking. The first burdens the decisionmaker with too much information while the second views information as of secondary importance. How, then, can a manager make decisions that are thoughtful and well researched but that do not overtax his ability to analyze information? Etzioni (1967) has given us a synthesis of the first two models called "limited rationality"—in Etzioni's words, "mixed scanning." In mixed scanning fundamental goals and directions are established through the pure rationality method, while day-to-day decisions are made by an incremental process, keeping in mind the organization's fundamental orientation. In turn, the commitments that result from the incremental decisions will play a part in the next review of the organization's fundamental decisions about its direction and goals. Figure 4–2 shows the three models of de-

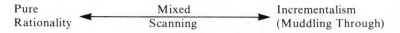

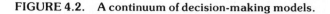

Pure   Mixed   Incrementalism
Rationality   ◄────────── Scanning ──────────►   (Muddling Through)

FIGURE 4.2.   A continuum of decision-making models.

cisionmaking along a continuum, with pure rationality and incrementalism at opposite ends.

Simon (1976) proposed a method of decisionmaking that reflects Etzioni's mixed scanning. He suggested that choices are always made with respect to a simplified model of the alternatives involved in the real situation. He also observed that search behavior is usually concerned only with *satisfactory* alternatives and only in exceptional cases with optimal alternatives. Finally, Simon said that continued failure to achieve a minimum standard of satisfaction results in successive lowering of the standard whereas easy success raises minimum standards.

The decisionmaker usually is faced with one of three knowledge situations, each of which has a typical response (Shull, Delbecq, and Cummings, 1970, p. 17):

1. Not enough information about variables. Individual chooses to drop the matter altogether. (This in itself is a decision.)
2. Not enough information, but individual knows more information is available. Search behavior ensues.
3. Not enough information, but individual is forced to arrive at decision because of time constraints.

Shull and his associates asserted that the third situation is most common in management decisions. One has to take a chance that an intelligent, albeit uncertain, action is better than no action at all. In the next section we shall examine criteria for good decisionmaking.

WHAT MAKES A GOOD DECISION PROCESS?

"There are no facts about the future," said former Secretary of Energy James Schlesinger in a speech. The future is indeed unknowable and every decision therefore involves some degree of risk. There are no right answers and, as Drucker (1977) said, there may not even be a range of optimums. An effective, proactive manager can only try to take the right risks. Drucker asserted that it is better to change a trend than to follow or even to anticipate it. What guidelines does a manager have to assess whether or not a decision is a good one? How is one to know whether a risk is reasonable? Janis and Mann (1977) have developed a useful list of seven criteria of high quality decisions based upon an extensive review of the decisionmaking literature, as well as their own research. They contend that a person's decisionmaking process is defective if any one of the seven criteria is not met. Furthermore, the extent to which the process is defective is the extent to which goals relating to the decision will not be met and the decisionmaker will experience regret and anxiety after the decision is made.

The decision maker, to the best of his ability and within his information-processing capabilities

1. thoroughly canvasses a wide range of alternative courses of action;
2. surveys the full range of objectives to be fulfilled and the values implicated by the choice;
3. carefully weighs whatever he knows about the costs and risks of negative consequences, as well as the positive consequences, that could flow from each alternative;
4. intensively searches for new information relevant to further evaluation of the alternatives;
5. correctly assimilates and takes account of any new information or expert judgment to which he is exposed, even when the information or judgment does not support the course of action he initially prefers;
6. reexamines the positive and negative consequences of all known alternatives, including those originally regarded as unacceptable, before making a final choice;
7. makes detailed provisions for implementing or executing the chosen course of action, with special attention to contingency plans that might be required if various known risks were to materialize. (p.11)

Janis and Mann have argued that each of the three models of decision-making discussed above meet these seven criteria. In their view, the key element of the criteria is information processing, the ability to search for and evaluate information relevant to all the alternatives to be considered. In the management of human services, program evaluators are valuable resources in this regard. It is the responsibility of the manager, though, to let the program evaluator know what questions need to be answered before decisions can be made (Broskowski, White, and Spector, 1979). For example, if one is considering starting a new program for a target group it is vital to ask the program evaluator specific questions, such as how many people in the target group are likely to use the prospective program in the geographical area to be served and how many people in the target group have been served by the organization's other programs in the past three months. If a program evaluator is asked vague questions for reasons that are not readily apparent, he is likely to supply vague information or information that is not relevant to the problem at hand. Information must be simple, accurate, timely, and to the point (Broskowski, White, and Spector, 1979; Wilder and Miller, 1973). It is up to the manager to let the program evaluator know precisely what the point is.

Asking the questions that generate ample and relevant information is most important in meeting Janis and Mann's criteria for a good decision. Their criteria, in turn, give managers one of the most useful guides available for evaluating the decisionmaking process and decisionmakers would do well to keep this checklist in mind. It is now time to review some relatively simple steps for actually making decisions.

MAKING UP YOUR MIND

There is no set formula for decisionmaking, no precise mixture of ingredients that all managers should use. Although a manager is assured of being on solid ground by paying attention to the seven criteria listed above, he still has a good deal of latitude in the exact manner in which he approaches each decision. There are, however, a few steps or stages, as indicated by the criteria, that one must go through with each decision. To begin, one must determine what the problem is. What is to be decided? Is there a standard procedure or a precedent that makes the question moot? A great deal of a manager's time is taken up making decisions that someone else thinks he should make when very often it would be more appropriate if ordinary procedures were followed. Sometimes the demand for a decision can be a coded message that something other than the question being posed should be examined. Also, the fact that the question is raised may be an indication that there is something wrong with the usual procedure (e.g., that it is obsolete) or that someone else has not done a job properly. For example, if one is continually being asked to make decisions about the details of the client intake procedure it may be that the procedure needs to be revised or has not been properly communicated. When the question to be decided is legitimate, the manager must determine what the relevant issues are. For example, if a manager is petitioned by subordinates to budget for new positions to accomplish routine tasks, he may determine that the real question is how to train the present staff to handle the workload in a more efficient and productive way.

Once the problem is defined the manager must begin the process of searching the environment for relevant information. In addition to gathering new information or retrieving existing information from stored data, he would do well to seek the opinions of colleagues and subordinates. At this stage the manager can elicit a wide variety of comments and opinions from anyone who has something to offer, an important process because implementation of the final choice is easier if everyone feels he had a say in the decisionmaking process. Also, the more people that are involved, the greater the chance that more useful information will be available to the manager and more alternatives for action will be identified.

The benefits of each alternative must be considered next. How do the benefits relate to the goals of the organization? In this regard it is useful to remember (and easy to forget) that human services organizations exist for clients, not the other way around. Similarly, the manager must consider the benefits of each alternative with regard to clinical services.

The risk of each alternative must also be carefully weighed at this stage. On the other hand, while it is always prudent to beware of risks, the fear of a bad outcome can paralyze a manager so that he makes only safe decisions. The inability to take risks threatens the vitality of the organization over time because bold, innovative action is needed to combat the effects of entropy (discussed in Chapter 2).

Timing is another key factor in decisionmaking. Sometimes it is useful to defer a decision. Conditions may change and the environment may be more conducive to a better outcome at a later time. Pascal could have been describing the environment of a decision when he wrote in his *Pensées*, "There is no man who differs more from another than he does from himself at another time." Once again, though, an indecisive manager and a reluctant decisionmaker can easily hide behind the excuse that "the time isn't right just now."

In human services management, where one has to deal with a myriad of constituencies, funding bodies, and interest groups, compromise is often the best solution. A friendly compromise may be possible without sacrificing organizational goals and the best interests of the agency's clients.

Finally, at some point a choice must be made. And here the manager stands alone, for committees don't make decisions. The manager alone has the authority to decide because he alone must bear responsibility for the outcome. More will be said about final choices and commitments in the next section. However, it is well to point out here that once a decision is made the manager has the right to expect that subordinates will do their best to support it even if they do not totally agree with it. Dissent is appropriate and indeed vital during the process of searching for alternatives before a choice is made. But dissent *following* the final choice can divide the staff and stir up discontent, which may damage worker morale and interfere with the delivery of services to clients.

Errors in decisionmaking arise when one or more of Janis and Mann's (1977) seven criteria are not met. There are, in addition, a few other causes of bad decisions. One is the biases and preconceived notions of the decisionmaker. If the decisionmaker determines at the beginning of the decisionmaking process what the decision will be, the search and deliberation stages will serve only to delude the decisionmaker—and everyone else—that all alternatives are receiving due consideration. To some extent, of course, preconceived notions play some part in the way we make decisions. The honest manager, however, should make every attempt to put prejudices out on the table so that he and his colleagues can deal with them and give other options a fair hearing.

Another pitfall is the fear of experimentation. Since the future is unknown, it is reasonable at times to try certain solutions even though some of them may fail. Franklin Delano Roosevelt tried many programs to end the Depression. Some, such as the National Recovery Administration (NRA) were failures; others, such as the Civilian Conservation Corps (CCC) and the bank closings were quite successful. Fortunately, the successes outweighed the failures.

Indecisiveness is yet another decisionmaking pitfall. When some decisions are deferred, especially those concerning pressing problems, tensions mount and the problems and all their spinoffs multiply. Additionally, undue hesitation may make the final decision more difficult to take.

Now that we have examined the decisionmaking process, we can turn our attention to implementation.

CHOICE AND COMMITMENT

Decisions find their utility in implementation. "Decisions must be action-oriented—that is, directed toward relevant and controllable aspects of the environment" (Shull, Delbecq, and Cummings, 1970, p. 12). Implementation is enhanced through the participation of all involved in the entire process—from definition of the problem to the final choice. Even though broad participation is important, everyone must understand that the final choice, and the responsibility for it, rests with the manager. As we have already seen, this responsibility is something that cannot be shared. The manager must be skillful at persuading others to accept a decision if they do not agree with it. This is done in a variety of ways, including co-optation of influential members of the informal network of communications and campaigning for support from the entire organization. But, if work group members feel ignored during the process of making decisions, there is little that will make them embrace the final choice.

Of course, the decisionmaker himself must be able fully to commit himself to the final choice. Mulling over the rightness or the wrongness of a decision after it has been made seems to be a good way to lose sleep and get ulcers. The danger here is that the manager, plagued by worries and conflicts, will dread and avoid future decisions. Kearns (1976) wrote that Lyndon Johnson envied the ability of Abraham Lincoln and Franklin Roosevelt to make momentous decisions without ever giving them a second thought, while he, like Herbert Hoover (one of his less impressive predecessors), fretted for days after making a decision.

We shall next discuss how information is exchanged and how decisions are communicated in organizations.

REFERENCES

BROSKOWSKI, A., WHITE, S. L., AND SPECTOR, P. "A management perspective on program evaluation." In H. C. Schulberg and J. Jerrell (eds.), *The Evaluator and Management*. Beverly Hills: Sage, 1979.

DROR, Y. *Public Policymaking Reexamined*. San Francisco: Chandler, 1967.

DRUCKER, P. *People and Performance*. New York: Harper & Row, 1977.

ETZIONI, A. "Mixed scanning: a third approach to decision-making." *Public Administration Review* (1967) 27(5):385–392.

HALBERSTAM, D. *The Best and the Brightest*. New York: Random House, 1972.

JANIS, I. L., AND MANN, L. *Decision Making*. New York: Free Press, 1977.

KAUFMAN, H. *The Forest Ranger: A Study in Administrative Behavior*. Baltimore: Johns Hopkins Press, 1967.

KEARNS, D. *Lyndon Johnson and the American Dream*. New York: Harper & Row, 1976.

LAVOIE, D. "The levels of logic managers use on the job." Paper presented at the annual conference of Administrative Sciences of Canada, University of Western Ontario, London, May 1978.

LEVINSON, D., AND KLERMAN, G. "The clinician-executive: some problematic issues for the psychiatrist in mental health organizations." *Psychiatry* (1967) 30(1): 3–15.

LINDBLOM, C. E. "The science of muddling through." *Public Administration Review* (1959) 19(2):79–99.

MINTZBERG, H. *The Nature of Managerial Work*. New York: Harper & Row, 1973.

PARKER, G. T. "While alma mater burns." *Atlantic Monthly* (1976) September: 39–47.

SHULL, F. A., DELBECQ, A. L., AND CUMMINGS, L. L. *Organizational Decision Making*. New York: McGraw-Hill, 1970.

SIMON, H. A. *Administrative Behavior*. 3d edition. New York: Free Press, 1976.

SORENSEN, T. C. *Decision-making in the White House*. New York: Columbia University Press, 1963.

THOMSON, J. D., AND TUDEN, A. "Strategies, structures, and processes of organizational decisions." In J. D. Thomson, P. B. Hammond, R. W. Hawkes, B. H. Junker, and A. Tuden (eds.), *Comparative Studies in Administration*. Pittsburgh: University of Pittsburgh Press, 1959.

TOWNSEND, R. *Up the Organization*. New York: Knopf, 1970.

WILDAVSKY, A. *The Politics of the Budgetary Process*. 2d edition. Boston: Little, Brown, 1974.

WILDER, J., AND MILLER, S. "Management information." In S. Feldman (ed.), *The Administration of Mental Health Services*. Springfield: Charles C Thomas, 1973.

Communicating

"What we have here is a failure to communicate" is the well-known line of the prison warden in the 1967 film *Cool Hand Luke*. Failures of communication are common in all organizations, and no less so in human services agencies that address many constituencies, employ several professions, and exhibit, in proportion to their size, great complexity. Communication is the process of moving information from a sender to a receiver in a way that insures that the receiver will understand the meaning intended by the sender. Organizations must be able to take in and process information to remain vital (Katz and Kahn, 1978). In this regard, managers must act as "information brokers" (Broskowski, White, and Spector, 1979; Cox, 1977; Mintzberg, 1973): they must see that information is communicated in a clear way so that the components of the organizations will be either integrated through shared information or differentiated through the delegation of specific responsibilities to various people in the organization. Facilitating information processing in order to integrate the components of an organization is one of the manager's major tasks. Through boundary-spanning communication, subsystems can work smoothly together. But even at a more prosaic level, managers must be able to communicate, among other things, instructions about tasks to be performed as well as information about such matters as scheduling, employee benefits, agency plans and policies, and the resolution of conflicts among individuals and groups.

In this chapter we shall examine several aspects of communication and information exchange in human services management. First I shall attempt to define communication and explain how it works in formal and informal organizations. We shall then move on to a discussion of the media of communication—oral and written—and a discussion of communication in interviews and committee meetings, tasks that are central in a manager's daily work. The chapter will end with an examination of some of the barriers to effective communication and will suggest how managers can overcome them.

WHAT IS COMMUNICATION?

Katz and Kahn (1978) defined communication as the exchange of information and the transmission of meaning. The sender of a message must be sure that the message is clear and easily understood and transmitted in such a way as to enhance its chance of being heard or read by its intended audience. Both the sender and the receiver must be aware of their shared responsibility for effective communication. While the sender of a message must be clear and precise, the receiver has the responsibility to let the sender know when he does not understand a message. Regarding the sender's responsibility in communicating, the essayist E. B. White (1962) told this story about Will Strunk, a legendary Cornell English professor of White's student days:

> Will felt that the reader was in serious trouble most of the time, a man floundering in a swamp, and that it was the duty of anyone attempting to write English to drain this swamp quickly and get his man up on dry ground, or at least throw him a rope. (p. 121)

In order to "drain the swamp" the sender must know where the swamp is and something about the floundering man. It is not enough simply to know your audience, as your high school English teacher probably advised. One must also know a good deal about the context within which the communication will take place. I say more about this later.

From an organizational perspective, communication is both fuel and lubricant. We have already seen that systems process information to achieve organizational goals. But the input of other resources (people, money, supplies), their transformation into services (health care, counseling, education), and the export of these outputs are also heavily dependent on communication. Reliable and timely information is needed to coordinate all of the functions of the various subsystems involved in these processes. Let us now look more closely at communication in organizations.

UP, DOWN, AND ACROSS

Formal communication follows the channels of supervision and authority depicted in the table of organization of the work setting. Many people think that formal communication is, by this definition, vertical (Lundgren,

Engel, and Cecil, 1978). This is, however, not necessarily the case. Formal communication may flow in a horizontal direction in a matrix organization (White, 1978) or to and from members of standing committees that represent the departments of an agency, hospital, or school. Also, horizontal communication takes place when two or more managers of equal stature in the hierarchy communicate with one another. In any case, formal communication is an important factor in understanding management and the ways in which organizations work. It is in the area of formal communication, especially along the vertical axis, that middle managers experience many of the vexations of being in the middle—between subordinates and top management. We shall take a directional approach to formal communication by looking at four types of communication.

"Downward communication" (see Figure 5-1) quite often concerns information from top management that middle managers must pass on to subordinates. It may also concern information that the middle manager

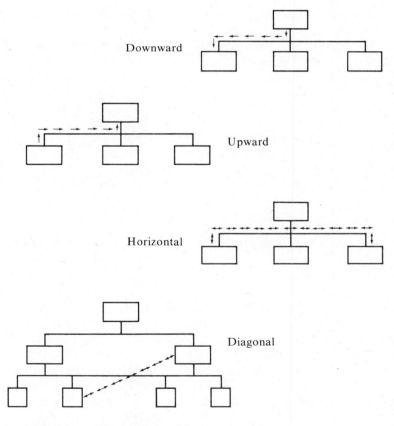

FIGURE 5.1.   Types of Formal Communication.

himself wishes to pass on to subordinates. Downward communication most often takes the form of directives that state policy or procedures, congratulate, advise, or warn. Sometimes downward communication is a response to requests for information from people lower in the hierarchy than the person to whom the request was made. Whatever the reason or source of downward communication, the middle manager must insure that the information be accurately interpreted and disseminated. A useful way of handling this problem is by passing a top manager's memorandum around in a staff meeting and carefully explaining its content and implications. In this way, workers see the original message and the manager can determine firsthand whether the message has been clearly understood.

Deciding whether information would be more effectively passed downward in writing or orally is a high art for which no good rules exist. In this area managers are frequently damned if they do and damned if they don't. Shortly after becoming a manager I passed information about a new procedure downward in the form of an informally written memorandum. Although important, the new procedure seemed innocuous to me. But I was severely criticized by my subordinates for being stuffy and making them feel "one down" from me by such an insensitive way of communicating. A few months later, remembering this incident, I passed another bit of information downward orally to the same group of workers at a staff meeting. A few weeks went by and the staff acted as though they had never received the message, which I thought had been thoroughly discussed at the meeting. When I asked the staff why no changes had been made, some said that the message had been unclear, others said they had not heard it, and one doubted my seriousness. Obviously, whether or not a message will be received by either the oral or the written approach depends heavily upon the content of the message, its tone, its timing, the relationship between the sender and the receivers, the ambiance of the organization at the particular time, and a host of other contextual factors. At best, as you gain experience, this problem will be ameliorated.

"Upward communication," the flow of information and messages from subordinates to managers, is generally more problematic than downward communication in most organizations for a variety of reasons. Workers may be intimidated by managers because of managers' stiffness or inaccessibility or because of unfounded (or valid) notions about how their messages will be received. They also may feel that they have been ignored or given inconsistent and confusing responses in the past. Finally, workers may believe that letting managers know too much may work to their disadvantage. Managers therefore must take a great deal of responsibility for facilitating upward communication. Without upward communication, a vital feedback loop is missing in the organization, and the consequences may be high staff turnover, low morale, low productivity, and poor quality services for clients.

The manager who wishes to stimulate upward communication must first attend to the morale of workers and to other factors having to do with the atmosphere of the workplace. A constricted, rigid atmosphere is not conducive to upward communication. Conversely, an atmosphere marked by excessive looseness makes for unclear, distorted, fragmented, and otherwise confusing messages. Weekly staff meetings at which important issues are openly discussed and debated will certainly enhance upward communication directly, as well as indirectly by improving morale. Other means, such as open-door policies, performance appraisal interviews, attitude surveys, grievance systems, suggestion systems, and formal and informal reports, will also stimulate upward communication.

"Horizontal communication," between people on the same level, and "diagonal communication," between people at different levels of the hierarchy but not in the same vertical line of authority, have much in common. They both make use of the formal organization, for example, when workers take part in a project in a matrix organization (horizontal) or when a line worker in a service department discusses retirement benefits with the director of personnel (diagonal). In situations like these all parties involved should keep their supervisors informed of any *formal* horizontal or diagonal contacts that are *not* of a routine nature. For example, the diagonal communication concerning retirement benefits would most probably be routine whereas communication between the same people concerning a grievance of the line worker would not. Keeping supervisors informed about nonroutine horizontal and diagonal communications avoids the tensions that may arise when a supervisor discovers that he is ignorant of certain information that affects his job and for which he is in some way responsible.

Informal horizontal and diagonal communication falls under the heading of the grapevine and has been discussed in other contexts in the first two chapters. It bears repeating, though, that the grapevine is a powerful and omnipresent element in any organization. The effective manager quickly finds ways to gain access to the grapevine so that he can make use of covert information that has not come to his attention by formal channels. Moreover, the manager may send messages via the grapevine that are more persuasive than formal communications.

THE SPOKEN WORD

If, as we have seen, communication is a sine qua non of organizational life, then the spoken word is its most common form. The greatest share of most managers' time, according to Mintzberg (1973), is spent in oral communication. Indeed, he found that managers spend fully 80 percent of their time in oral contacts—telephone calls, one-to-one conversations, and scheduled or unscheduled meetings. Because of their preference for action and a fast moving pace, managers seem to prefer oral communication, sometimes at their peril. Oral communication can lead to two problems: information overload and superficiality.

Information overload occurs when a person (or a computer, a group of people, or a formal organization) takes in more information than he can process. We saw in Chapter 4 that information overload can lead to faulty decisionmaking because the overwhelmed decisionmaker cannot make use of all the pertinent information involved in the question to be resolved. With 80 percent of his time spent in oral communication, the manager constantly risks this kind of overload. Although information overload can occur in the written medium, memoranda, letters, journal articles, and notes can be sorted, stored, and retrieved in an orderly fashion that allows the manager a little more time to be attentive to the full implications of the information than does the oral medium. Oral communication can be easily forgotten or misinterpreted whereas written communication can clarify meanings and remind all parties of past understandings and future commitments.

When information overload occurs, as it often does, information will not receive sufficient attention (Ackoff, 1967) and superficiality may result. One method for dealing with this problem is to employ a modified open-door policy whereby subordinates are welcome to drop by to discuss problems at specified times during the week with the stipulation that they have the problems they want to discuss clearly defined in their minds *before* they come in. This policy not only controls access but also forces subordinates to think problems out, oftentimes obviating a manager's intervention.

When a manager is overwhelmed by a constant barrage of bits and fragments of information, he may attempt to deal swiftly with each fragment so that pressure for definitive action may be reduced or put off. In this way he may tend to concern himself only with parts of the organization's total life. This superficiality severely limits a manager's ability to anticipate and plan for problems.

Using the oral medium in their daily work, managers must translate "information into action—or at least into actionable instructions for subordinates" (Hollander, 1978, p. 119). They must also keep information flowing and continually clarify their own meanings and ask for clarification from others. This issue becomes clouded when we consider other aspects of oral communication such as gestures, tone of voice, and facial expressions. These "metacommunications"—communications *about* communications —are powerful elements of any oral exchange. Gestures and facial expressions, for example, can support and strengthen a manager's oral message or they can disqualify or blunt his message. What is at stake in the realm of metacommunication is not only clarity and the manager's true meaning but also his perceived sincerity and integrity. One must strive for consistency.

THE WRITTEN WORD

Given the limitations of the spoken word, written communication takes on a great deal of importance in an organization. A large part of a manager's job is writing and responding to letters, memoranda, and reports. Few managers enjoy this part of their work and fewer still can say, as Winston Churchill did in his autobiography, that if they learned nothing else in their early years at school they at least learned how to write a good English sentence. While writing does not come easily to many people, with a little effort one can learn the basics of good writing and so improve one's ability to communicate. To begin, a new manager should carefully read *the Elements of Style* by Will Strunk and E. B. White (1979). In a clear, concise, and entertaining manner, this little book presents the essentials of good writing. It has excellent, short chapters on usage, composition, form, and commonly misused words and expressions and contains a superb short piece on the essentials of developing a clear writing style.

Whether he is writing a letter to the family of a client, a memorandum about a new method of keeping client records, or a grant proposal to start a pilot project for counseling children at risk for learning disabilities, the manager-writer must keep two things in mind: purpose and audience.

First, let us consider purpose. Why are you writing that letter or memo or grant proposal? As indicated earlier, writing when speaking would do can get one into trouble. It is important both to be sure that writing is the best medium for the intended message and to know clearly what the main idea or core purpose of the message is. A piece of writing with no clear purpose, or several ill-defined purposes, will either dilute the meaning of the intended message or bore the reader so much that he will divert his attention to something more interesting. Additionally, a clear understanding of the purpose of a piece of writing will help the writer determine what should be included and what should be omitted.

The second thing a manager-writer must keep in mind is his audience. Who is being addressed? Who will read what is being written? Certainly an informal memo to staff about a change in procedure will differ in tone from a letter to a client or a letter of reprimand to a wayward subordinate. A grant seeker will want to know something about the people who will review his proposal and the program priorities of the funding agency so that he can slant his writing in a way that offers the best chance of getting his proposal funded. While jargon of any kind should always be avoided, it is particularly inappropriate if the audience does not belong to the group in which the jargon would be readily understood.

After a writer has stated his purpose and decided who his audience is, he must attend to organization, sorting out ideas and ordering them in a logical way. For example, a memo explaining the intake procedure in a public assistance agency or the method of inserting a new kind of intravenous needle should begin with the most basic step and proceed in a logical, point-by-point manner. Or, when analyzing a problem, each part of the problem should be identified and discussed in turn.

There are other aspects of good writing that a manager-writer should keep in mind. One pitfall to avoid, especially common in the writings of social scientists and human services professionals, is the passive voice:

> Staff members are asked to turn in their daily activity logs to the receptionist.

is less forceful than

> Staff members should turn in their daily activity logs to the receptionist.

Something to strive for in good writing is brevity. Wordiness, or overwriting, will put off readers.

Dictating is another hazard for the manager-writer. Recording devices of all kinds are gaining in popularity in human services agencies, as they have in business and industry. Few people seem to realize that dictating requires them carefully to organize their thoughts and words before they commit themselves on tape. Therefore, anything that has been dictated should be carefully revised before a final copy is typed. Rewriting is a good idea in any kind of writing but is imperative when the first draft has been dictated because people are generally less precise when they speak than when they write something out by hand.

Besides all that the manager has to write, there is an enormous amount of information that he must read or at least *thinks* he must read. There are notes and memos from top management and managers in other departments, computer and manual reports on productivity and quality assurance, requests for personal and administrative leaves, professional journals and books, letters from clients and other agencies, new standards and regulations from funding bodies and government agencies, and much more to tax the harried manager. Once again, the issue of information overload arises: how can a manager, who must be concerned with a variety of other tasks, attend to the glut of reading material so that what he reads has some meaning to him? The answer, with a few exceptions, is that he cannot attend to all of it. He must, to borrow Etzioni's (1967) term, engage in "mixed scanning"; that is, he must read selectively so that what is important is attended to and what is not is deferred. Some basic time management techniques are helpful in this regard. For example, one or two hours per day uninterrupted by telephone calls and meetings should be devoted to reading. Each day every letter, memo, report, and other piece of written communication should be sorted into roughly four piles: (1) *action*—must be handled that day; (2) *review*—should be handled within a week but is not urgent; (3) *file*—important information that may be needed at a later date but is not urgent; and (4) *discard*—this is the stuff that piles up because you'll never get to it, but you won't admit it.

Once everything is sorted, the manager can turn his attention to that day's action pile. When this is finished, the manager can get to the review pile to keep it down to a reasonable size. With a little practice you will be able to read that article on national health insurance or biofeedback that you have been meaning to get to. The key to this way of handling reading material is a helpful secretary who sees that you are left alone, a little self-discipline, and the honesty to admit that you cannot and will not be able to read everything that comes your way.

One final word about reading: in reading the action and review piles, learn to look for main ideas contained in topic sentences and summary statements. Most of the time it is unnecessary to read every word. Skimming and other fast reading techniques are easily learned and should be used.

INTERVIEWS AND MEETINGS

A great deal of communication takes place in interviews and meetings with one or more people. In these contacts, communication is enhanced by employing basic listening skills, which should have been learned by human services professionals long before they became managers. Nevertheless, a few major points should be emphasized. It is important to listen carefully and actively to the speaker. One should ask for clarification if he becomes vague and ask him to restate his purpose and focus on it if he gets off the track. Also, one should try to maintain eye contact. In spite of how painfully boring some people can be, it is best to concentrate and avoid the temptation to let your mind wander to other things. This is especially true when significant but complicated and uninteresting material is being discussed. It is also important to be open to information that is unpleasant to hear or with which one does not agree. (Remember that Lyndon Johnson did not like hearing what a mess things were in Vietnam because it distracted him from his interest in domestic policy. So, his military aides started telling him that everything was fine in Vietnam.)

In formal staff meetings it is generally a good idea to have someone take notes so that minutes of the meeting are available to participants. Minutes or notes should also be taken when there are disputes or disagreements. Of course, note taking should be employed judiciously since recording what is said may *contribute* to the tension or even cause it. Finally, minutes and memoranda allow all the participants in an interview or meeting to come to agreement about what was said and what action is to be taken by whom.

OVERCOMING BARRIERS TO COMMUNICATION

There are many barriers to communication and many ways to overcome them. In some of the preceding sections we discussed a few barriers to effective communication, such as information overload, and reviewed ways to surmount them. In this final section of the chapter several other barriers will be reviewed.

1. *Lack of clarification* is probably the most common obstacle to effective communication. When the meaning of the person with whom you are communicating is not clear to you, ask him for clarification. And continually ask your listeners whether your meaning is clear to them.

2. *Inconsistent messages* are confusing and distracting. They can be avoided with some thought and planning so that communications in the form of instructions and procedures are consistent and right the first time they are stated, obviating the need for later modifications or retractions.

3. The *distance* between the sender and the receiver of messages is a major obstacle to good communication. The physical or psychological distance between, for example, the main office and a satellite center or even between two floors in the same building can severely limit the quality and quantity of the communication that goes on between the two parties. The manager can bridge this gap by making frequent visits to his far-flung jurisdictions and by setting up formal and informal mechanisms so that workers from the various workplaces meet and discuss their work on a regular basis.

4. *Heterogeneity*, as discussed by Kaufman (1967), refers to differences in professional or technical orientations between and among the various disciplines and technologies represented in the work environment. Most professions have their own jargon, a special problem in general hospitals and multiservice centers that provide a range of health, social, economic, and educational services. For example, program evaluators and psychotherapists in a community mental health center sometimes speak in entirely different languages (Broskowski, White, and Spector, 1979). All concerned in these interdisciplinary situations should avoid jargon and take pains to speak and write in plain English.

5. Related to heterogeneity is *perception*. Depending upon the audience, the subject under discussion, the ambiance of the workplace, vested interests, and a host of other contextual factors, different people may have distinct and sometimes conflicting perceptions about what is said and what is agreed upon. Constant efforts at clarification, followed by written memoranda of understanding, may bring all participants in a given exchange of information to a common perception of meaning.

6. *Ambiguity* can cause a message to have several quite different meanings. In this connection, Henderson and Soujanen (1974) retold the well-known English joke about three men riding in a train:

> First man: "Is this Wembley?"
> Second man: "No, today's Thursday."
> Third man: "So am I. Let's get off and have a drink." (p.62)

Repeating the message and offering sufficient clarification should remedy the problem of ambiguity.

Now that we have discussed communication and other skills of leadership and decisionmaking, we shall turn our attention to some specific tasks of management. The first we shall deal with, and one of the most problematic, is planning.

REFERENCES

ACKOFF, R. "Management information systems." *Management Science* (1967) 14(4):B147–B156.

BROSKOWSKI, A., WHITE, S. L., AND SPECTOR, P. "A management perspective on program evaluation." In H. C. SCHULBERG AND J. JERRELL (eds.), *The Evaluator and Management*. Beverly Hills: Sage, 1979.

COX, G. B. "Managerial style: implications for the utilization of program evaluation information." *Evaluation Quarterly* (1977) 1(3):499–508.

ETZIONI, A. "Mixed scanning: a third approach to decision-making." *Public Administration Review* (1967) 27(5):385–392.

HENDERSON, R. I., AND SOUJANEN, W. W. *The Operating Manager*. Englewood Cliffs: Prentice-Hall, 1974.

HOLLANDER, E. P. *Leadership Dynamics*. New York: Free Press, 1978.

KATZ, D., AND KAHN, R. L. *The Social Psychology of Organizations*. 2d edition. New York: Wiley, 1978.

KAUFMAN, H. *The Forest Ranger: A Study in Administrative Behavior*. Baltimore: Johns Hopkins Press, 1967.

LUNDGREN, E. F., ENGEL, W. J., AND CECIL, E. A. *Supervision*. Columbus: Grid, 1978.

MINTZBERG, H. *The Nature of Managerial Work*. New York: Harper & Row, 1973.

STRUNK, W., AND WHITE, E. B. *The Elements of Style*. 3rd edition. New York: Macmillan, 1979.

WHITE, E. B. *The Points of My Compass*. New York: Harper, 1962.

WHITE, S. L. "The community mental health center as a matrix organization." *Administration in Mental Health* (1978) 6(2):99–106.

The Planning Process

The scene is a crowded sandwich shop in a mid-size American city. It is noontime and the shop is crowded with human services professionals from neighboring offices and agencies on lunch break. Within a three-block radius of the shop there is a 400-bed general hospital, a state welfare office, a public high school, and two storefront clinics and social services agencies. As we move around the crowded shop looking for a table, we hear fragments of conversation:

"Yeah, I know what you mean. I spend all my time putting out fires, too!"

"We had to drop everything this week to get a grant proposal written. It's due on Friday, but my boss knew about it three weeks ago and has just been sitting on it."

"Today is my first day back from vacation, and what a mess I found! Seems as though the place couldn't function at all without me. Nobody knew how to handle simple problems and nothing got done."

"Our new satellite office opens up next week and nobody knows any of the details yet."

"So I said to her, 'Jackie, that's a great idea, but how does it fit in with the rest of our program?' "

These snatches of conversation are evidence that the professionals and managers at the sandwich shop are engaged in a favorite luncheon pastime, often called "Ain't it awful!" The version of the game being played in the shop is particularly popular in organizations where little short- or long-range planning is done. An understanding of planning is crucial for new managers simply because change in organizations is a constant phenomenon. The manager has two choices regarding this phenomenon: either he can allow the changing environment to manage him and be satisfied with the results, whatever they are, or he can anticipate and adapt to the changing environment in ways that accomplish his own and the organization's goals. It will not be a surprise to learn that the second choice is advocated here for, as Goethe reminds us, "to live is to adapt."

To adapt in a proactive way that exploits environmental changes to the best advantage of the organization's goals requires constant vigilance and constant attention to the future. In organizations, the beginning of adaptation to change is planning. Littlestone (1973) defined planning as

> a process that begins with setting objectives; then defining strategies, policies and detailed plans to achieve them; establishing an organization to implement decisions, and reviewing performance and feedback to introduce a new planning cycle. (p. 5)

and later as

> deciding in advance what is to be done, when it is to be done, how it is to be done, and who is to do it. [This process] is continuous because changes in the environment are continuous. (p. 5–6)

Some basic assumptions about planning should be stated before going on. Of primary importance is the assumption that organizations can be improved, to the benefit of clients and staff, by sustained and clearly focused action by middle and lower level staff members (Brager and Holloway, 1978; Resnick, 1977; Weissman, 1973). Another assumption is that planning is a dynamic, continuous activity that influences, and is influenced by, all of the interacting elements of the organization. A third assumption is that a program's goals must be clearly formulated and sanctioned by higher authority in the organization before planning can begin. Accurate and timely information about all matters touching on the program's intended goals is crucial to the planning process. Finally, everyone involved in the program should take part in the planning process for the dual purpose of generating appropriate ideas and information and reducing resistance to the changes that are planned. With these assumptions in mind we shall now attempt to answer the question "How do you know when you should begin the planning process?"

SCANNING THE ENVIRONMENT

One answer to this question has already been suggested. A good manager is *always* planning: the process never stops. For the purpose of this chapter, however, we shall consider planning as a formal process that has an identifiable beginning and end. And, as one might expect, the beginning of the planning process depends on circumstances in the environment. Environment is defined here as the total context—social, political, fiscal, professional, community, historical, etc.—in which the program in question operates. The environment of a human services program within a larger agency includes, but is not limited to, the agency's administration, major sources of funding, interest groups in the community, and trends and developments in the technology of the services being provided.

The board of directors and the executive director the board hires are ultimately responsible for everything that happens in a human services agency. Furthermore, the executive director is responsible for integrating the agency's programs in a way that fits the overall philosophy and mission of the agency. The task of integrating programs is made difficult by the tendency of the programs to differentiate themselves by establishing autonomous identities (Lawrence and Lorsch, 1967; Young, 1979). While a certain amount of autonomy is probably necessary for a staff's enthusiasm for a particular program, moving too far out of the orbit of the parent agency can be dangerous since programs must compete for the agency's total but scarce resources. A program that is so differentiated from other programs within an agency may be seen by the executive director an inconsistent with the objectives of the organization as a whole. For this reason a manager should be continually aware of the programmatic priorities of the agency's board of directors and executive director. If these priorities are not explicitly stated by the administration, the manager must work all the harder to discover the agency's covert priorities. A manager who develops plans for a program that conflict with the programmatic priorities of the agency's administration will, after much frustration, meet with little success. So, the effort to discover these priorities is well worth it.

In this context, it is important to note that priorities of one program may conflict with the priorities of other programs. This is especially true when the missions of the programs in question are ill-defined or vague. It is also true when several programs are competing for scarce resources. The phenomenon of conflicting priorities can exist within a single program. For example, given a finite budget, the staff of a program may clamor for salary increases but at the same time be unwilling to cut costs elsewhere in the program's budget to allow for the increases. This situation can be enormously frustrating to a manager.

Agency priorities comprise an important part of the internal environment. The remainder of this discussion will be concerned with the agency's external environment. The first aspect we shall consider involves money. A program will increase its chance of being funded to the extent that it conforms to the priorities of government funding agencies at the federal, state, and local levels. State and local funding priorities often follow the priorities of the federal government since a great deal of state and local funds come from federal sources. For example, mental health program priorities in most state and local jurisdictions for the early 1980s will probably conform to many of the recommendations of President Carter's Commission on Mental Health, which made its final report in April 1978. A mental health program manager therefore would be on solid ground, for instance, in planning to expand services for the chronically mentally ill—a high priority of the president's commission and the Mental Health Systems Act, which resulted from the commission's work.

There are many ways to scan an organization's external environment. For example, by reading newsletters of national human services professional organizations and other publications related to national health, education, and welfare legislation, a manager can usually predict what the federal funding priorities will be for his areas of interest over the coming few years. In like manner, one should make an effort to be continually aware of the funding priorities of other current or potential funding sources for one's programs such as the United Way, religious organizations, and private foundations.

In order to be successful, a human services program must be accepted and supported by the community it seeks to serve. It is not enough for the community to *need* a service; it must also *want* the service. In 1977 the Northside Community Mental Health Center in Tampa, Florida, wanted to open a satellite outpatient office in an affluent neighborhood as part of an effort to generate more revenue. Before going ahead with the project the center canvassed the neighborhood to determine the extent of the need for mental health outpatient services. The residents of the neighborhood were asked under what circumstances they would use the services of the community mental health center. The survey revealed that the *need* for the service was quite high. Nevertheless, the ability of the affluent residents to purchase private mental health services, perceived to be of higher quality, made the estimated *demand* for the community mental health center's services too low to warrant risking the expense of opening a new office in that neighborhood. Thus, this satellite clinic was abandoned. A manager must be sensitive to a variety of other issues regarding community acceptance of a program. A good example involves the efforts of some neighborhoods to enforce or rewrite city zoning regulations that would prohibit the opening of group homes for the mentally retarded or for juvenile delinquents. It is ironic that programs designed to improve the human condition often set off a series of reactions nearly as troublesome as the problems the programs seek to remedy. As the television commentator Eric Sevareid once said, "The chief cause of problems is solutions."

Program planning in the human services should depend on the state of the art of the program's core technology. For example, in the 1960s curriculum planning in many regions was dominated by humanistic thinking, which led to the adoption of the open classroom concept in elementary schools. The open classroom had a major effect not only on curriculum planning but also on school construction and teacher education. Similarly, the advent of psychopharmacology in the 1950s enabled chronic mental patients to live outside state hospitals for longer periods of time than had ever before been possible. This development in turn led to more and more community based mental health programs, which have almost totally eclipsed the old state hospitals. Managers must keep abreast of developments in their field by reading journals, attending conferences, and visiting agencies where new ideas are being tried out. Once again, the information explosion and constant changes in our understanding of health, education, and social welfare technology make this task never ending. However, in addition to keeping abreast of developments in technology, remember that in the human services ideology is often disguised as technology. The manager must have technical expertise to tell the difference between emerging technology and the latest fad.

As we have seen, the manager in the role of program planner must be aware of a variety of constraints. But he must also be alert to a wide range of opportunities. Keeping close contact with federal, state, and local legislators and agency officials will give one an advantage in securing resources and in learning about opportunities for grants and other types of support for programs. Community leaders and local civic clubs and organizations are often eager to support a new human services project. Also, government publications, particularly the *Congressional Record*, are a regular source of program funding opportunities.

When environmental changes are seen as a threat, as something bad, the organization's ability to adapt is impaired. On the other hand, environmental changes can be viewed as unique opportunities to be seized and exploited in an open and aggressive manner. This second strategy marks organizations that survive while the first marks those that ultimately fail.

THINKING AND BRAINSTORMING

It seems self-evident that thinking is a necessary precursor of planning. So, why mention it? Because managers spend too little time reflecting about their programs and the ways their programs fit into the whole agency's scheme of things. Mintzberg (1973) noted managers' preference for live action and for nonroutine events:

> The pressure of the managerial environment does not encourage the development of reflective planners, the classical literature notwithstanding. The job breeds adaptive information-manipulators who prefer the live concrete situation. The manager works in an environment of stimulus-response, and he develops in his work a clear preference for live action. (p. 38)

This description, accurate as it may be, does not free the manager of the responsibility to be reflective about the current state of his program or plans for its future. Too often plans are implemented with no thought given to possible unintended consequences. These consequences may subvert the organization's primary purpose or create a myriad of problems that will prove difficult to control.

Some of the things that the manager must consider carefully as he approaches the planning process are the fit between the intended program and the total agency's philosophy and direction; the possible resistance to change from subordinates; the costs and sources of support for the intended program; and the ways in which the intended program may positively or adversely affect the organization's relationships with people and organizations inside and outside the parent agency. If potential problems in any of these areas are not identified before planning begins, progress from goal setting to implementation will almost certainly not be smooth. Taking the time to reflect about the intended program is a good way to clear the deck of at least some potential obstacles.

The manager who has carefully thought through the problem at hand and formulated possible solutions (and considered the possible consequences of these solutions) constitutes what Resnick (1977) called the "change catalyst." The change catalyst's next task, according to Resnick, is to convene the "action system" to begin working on innovations. Groups are almost always more effective problem-solvers than are individuals, so the more people in the action system, up to a maximum of eight to ten, the more ideas will be generated. It is the job of the action system to brainstorm about what the problem is, what the goals and objectives of the program should be, and what the specific plans for the program should be. The following nine guidelines have proved useful in convening action systems for brainstorming:

1. Pick a diverse group to insure a variety of ideas and approaches.
2. Call the action system by a special name to convey a sense of its importance. Names such as "special task force" or "study group" or "ad hoc committee" can be effective if not overused.
3. Set up a special meeting with a clearly defined issue to discuss and determine ahead of time what will *not* be discussed.
4. Limit the length of the meeting to no more than ninety minutes so that group members will be forced to focus on the problem.
5. Encourage a free flow of ideas. In the brainstorming phase the quantity of ideas is more important than the quality.
6. Get everyone to speak up and express ideas. Record the ideas for later reference.
7. Mingle and modify ideas and begin to move toward a consensus after everyone has had a chance to make suggestions.
8. Keep rolling with ideas; don't zero in on early ideas that are appealing; and, above all, don't make any decisions.
9. Appoint a "judgment group" of no more than three persons, including the manager, to distill ideas further. The members of the judg-

ment group should have access to budget information so that they can know what is financially possible and what is not.

Committees do not make decisions; individuals do. The manager should use all of the recommendations of the action system and the judgment group to arrive at decisions about the precise course the planning process will take. At later stages in the planning process it will be useful to reconvene the action system to formulate specific procedures and methods of activity for the new program.

SOME MODELS OF PROGRAM PLANNING

There is no one best way to plan a program. As with so much else in management, the planning process depends on the people involved, the task to be accomplished, and the environment of the organization. There are a few models of planning, however, that illustrate the essential components of the process. One of the best known planning models in human services circles is called A VICTORY and was developed by Howard R. Davis at the National Institute of Mental Health (Larsen, 1973). A VICTORY is an acronym designed to call to mind the important factors to consider in planning change (Larsen, 1973, p. 3):

A Ability - What are your resources and capabilities?
V Values - Does the idea match your styles and beliefs?
I Information - How do you find out about things?
C Circumstances - What is your environment like?
T Timing - Is this the time to try it?
O Obligation - Is there motivation to change?
R Resistances - What problems can you expect?
Y Yield - What is the reward for changing?

The elements of the A VICTORY model are used to work through each of the four general steps in planning change:

1. Analysis: Background work, thinking, and brainstorming.
2. Goal definition: Identification of hoped for outcomes.
3. Action: Development of procedures and their implementation.
4. Follow-through: Prevention of regression to pre-change conditions and evaluation of the outcome.

For the purpose of the model these sequences are broken down as discrete entities. In reality, however, they overlap. All of the sequences should be present in the planning process according to this model.

Two other models of program planning come from the field of education, in which the development of curricula is a fundamental task for teachers and educational administrators. Lapp and Flood (1978) begin the curriculum planning process by surveying existing curriculum structures and by assessing the ideas and needs of administrators, teachers, parents, and children. They then generate operational themes that fit the interests and abilities of the children. In this stage they are concerned with whatever will gain acceptance with the children *and* achieve objectives. The next step is setting general objectives and, from these, determining specific behavioral objectives that can be measured. At the implementation stage the children are preassessed, taught, and posttested.

McNeil (1977), also an educator, developed a four-stage curriculum planning model:

1. Determine curriculum ends (objectives).
2. Develop curriculum means (actual course of instruction).
3. Implement curriculum.
4. Evaluate results of the curriculum.

McNeil echoed other planners when he noted that in developing a curriculum a teacher must consider several constituencies including, but not limited to, parents, principal, school board, federal and state education officials, pressure groups, and, of course, the children.

Littlestone (1973), quoted earlier in this chapter, identified the four elements of planning that seem to be common to most, if not all, models of program planning. He observed that the planning process must concern itself with:

1. Objectives.
2. Strategies, policies, and detailed plans.
3. Implementation.
4. Review and feedback.

The first two steps listed here will be discussed in the remainder of this chapter. The third will be discussed in Chapters 7, 8, and 10. Step four will be covered in detail in Chapter 9.

TYPES OF PLANS

There are basically two types of plan: "standing plans" and "single-use plans." Standing plans concern routine activities of a program and are subdivided into policies, procedures, and methods. "Policies" are "broad guidelines to action" (Lundgren, Engel, and Cecil, 1978, p. 74). Well-defined policies allow workers to take independent action without continually checking with their supervisors. Policies set the bounds of workers' discretion and eliminate the need for managers to make routine decisions. New policies should be communicated to workers orally and in writing, and they should be updated yearly.

"Procedures" are more specific than policies and usually describe the way an activity should be carried out in chronological order. For example, most human services agencies have intake procedures that describe in detail the steps a person must go through to receive services from the initial telephone call, to being interviewed by the business office, to meeting with the professional who will provide the service. Most employers also have something called a "grievance procedure," which details the steps a worker can go through to appeal action taken by a supervisor.

"Methods" are the precise directions for one of the steps under procedures. They tell exactly how a particular activity should be carried out. For example, student nurses are taught early in their training methods of keeping a wound or a surgical site sterile and methods for bandaging certain parts of the body.

Standing plans, with all their components, do not have to be developed for every single function and activity of a program. Too many rules and regulations and prescriptions for doing things can stifle workers and the entire organization. Some functions are quite complicated and lend themselves to error, however, and should be governed by written plans that are understood by new employees.

Single-use plans are developed for nonrecurring events such as special projects and conferences. Single-use plans are also developed to outline the process by which a new program will be put together and by which its new standing plans will be drawn up. These plans should relate to the objectives and policies of the program and its parent agency.

RETURN TO STABILITY

This chapter has dealt with planning for change; it will end with a note of caution about the effects of uncontrolled change. Toffler (1970) described the overwhelming societal implications of the technological revolution and concluded that mankind must "undertake the control of change, the guidance of his evolution" (p. 487) in order to avoid the consequences of "future shock." Sarason (1972) pointed out that many organizations are failing today partly because their leaders do not stabilize and maintain these organizations after the excitement of their creation has subsided. In their provocative paper on managing change and stability, Broskowski, Mermis, and Khajavi (1975) wrote, "all systems require a dynamic interplay between change *and* stability for successful growth" (p. 1). They observed that effective and lasting change in systems usually occurs in short phases of change and growth followed by relatively long periods of stability, which are necessary for high productivity because the change process uses up energy otherwise consumed through productivity.

Broskowski and co-workers (1975) coined the term "stay agent" to describe the person(s) whose behaviors restore an organization to stability after a period of rapid change. The stay agent has three important tasks. The first of these is the building and maintaining of the new organization's boundaries. This is done by promoting high morale and esprit de corps based upon common goals and expectations. The stay agent's second task is the building of internal networks between his and other subsystems in the agency. The new program must be linked and coordinated with other service programs in the agency to insure continuity of service. It also must be effectively linked to the business office, management information system, client records department, and other support subsystems in the agency. Collecting and maintaining new resources is the third, and most important, task of the stay agent. He must recruit new members for the organization and insure its continued financial and community support. In a very real sense, he must be the gatekeeper of the system's boundary in order to screen out disruptive elements. While the organization needs a variety of inputs to remain viable, the stay agent must see to it that the new elements do not exceed the organization's "ability to absorb and cope with the turbulent elements" (Broskowski, Mermis, and Khajavi, 1975, p. 3). Too much variety will fragment the organization and divert it from its goals.

THINGS TO REMEMBER

The planning process is usually complicated. For that reason I will conclude this chapter by stating, and in some cases reviewing, some of the most important ideas that a planner must keep in mind. Demone and Harshbarger (1973) asserted that the effectiveness of planning depends upon the involvement and cooperation of the target community; the participation of the professionals involved; and the sagacity of planners when faced with many attractive alternatives in a turbulent environment. Planners must resist the temptation to run off in all directions simultaneously.

Participation of professionals, as has already been mentioned several times, is crucial to implementation. In order to involve skeptical and phlegmatic professionals the manager must demonstrate clearly the need for change and the ways that the change will benefit the professionals. If the planning task is seen as valuable and made to appear enjoyable and exciting, the manager will have an easier time engaging professionals in the process. Once they are engaged, they must be listened to and must never be made to feel that their involvement is tokenism. The manager must be prepared to step aside as natural leaders in the planning group emerge. He must retain veto power (and make it clear that he is doing so) but must hold the reins loosely. He must also make it clear that in any process of change there are trade-offs. Even good changes can distress people. The manager must deal forthrightly with the drawbacks as well as the advantages of changes.

Finally, the manager who is concerned with the vitality and long-range future of his program will constantly be on the alert for ways the program can be improved by being more responsive to its client population. At times this means an expansion of the program; at other times this means a total refocusing of the program as when, for example, the March of Dimes redefined its mission once polio was eradicated. Complacency, on the other hand, will over time cause the program to become more and more rigid and less and less responsive to clients.

We shall now turn our attention to developing and managing a program budget and to managing finances in the human services, the first step in implementing plans.

REFERENCES

BRAGER, G., AND HOLLOWAY, S. *Changing Human Service Organizations.* New York: Free Press, 1978.

BROSKOWSKI, A., MERMIS, W. L., AND KHAJAVI, F. "Managing the dynamics of change and stability." In J. E. Jones and J. W. Pfeiffer (eds.), *The 1975 Annual Handbook for Group Facilitators*. La Jolla, California: University Associates, 1975.

DEMONE, H. W., AND HARSHBARGER, D. "The planning and administration of human services." In H. Schulberg, F. Baker, and S. Roen (eds.), *Developments in Human Services*. New York: Behavioral Publications, 1973.

LAPP, D., AND FLOOD, J. *Teaching Reading to Every Child*. New York: Macmillan, 1978.

LARSEN, J. K. *Planning for Change*. Palo Alto: American Institutes for Research, 1973.

LAWRENCE, P., AND LORSCH, J. "Differentiation and integration in complex organizations." *Administrative Science Quarterly* (1967) 12(1):1–47.

LITTLESTONE, R. "Planning in mental health." In S. Feldman (ed.), *The Administration of Mental Health Services*. Springfield: Charles C Thomas, 1973.

LUNDGREN, E. F., ENGEL, W. J., AND CECIL, E. A. *Supervision*. Columbus: Grid, 1978.

MINTZBERG, H. *The Nature of Managerial Work*. New York: Harper & Row, 1973.

McNEIL, J. D. *Curriculum: A Comprehensive Introduction*. Boston: Little, Brown, 1977.

RESNICK, H. "Effecting internal change in human service organizations." *Social Casework* (1977) 58(9):546–553.

SARASON, S. *The Creation of Settings and the Future Societies*. San Francisco: Jossey-Bass, 1972.

Toffler, A. *Future Shock*. New York: Random House, 1970.

Weissman, H. H. *Overcoming Mismanagement in the Human Service Professions*. San Francisco: Jossey-Bass, 1973.

Young, D. W. *The Managerial Process in Human Service Agencies*. New York: Praeger, 1979.

Managing Money

If it is true that clinical training is inadequate preparation for management, nowhere is this more true than in financial management. Planning for the procurement and use of resources is crucial to the success, indeed to the very existence, of organizations. Yet financial management is an area that clinical managers often avoid as if their integrity would be sullied if they were to deal in so base a thing as money. And then there are those who have no fears about their integrity but who are mystified by the apparent labyrinth of budgeting and financial jargon and feel that the entire subject is beyond them.

No manager can avoid dealing with issues of financial management; budgeting and managing money are basic to managerial work. Those managers who think of financial issues as bothersome imponderables will be addressed in this chapter. True enough, the area is complicated, because, as with any system, it is vulnerable to a constantly shifting environment that sets off a host of interconnected changes. But there are certain key concepts, which are not so complicated, that should be familiar to any manager at any level of the organization. We shall begin our discussion of financial management by defining budgets and reviewing the various types of budgets. Next we shall examine a typical budget cycle and go through the steps of preparing a budget for a small program in a mental health agency. Finally, we shall review how a budget can be used throughout the fiscal year as a management tool to monitor a program's progress toward attaining goals.

WHAT IS A BUDGET?

A budget is nothing more than a plan of action, usually for one year's duration, expressed in the numbers of dollars required to reach the goals the organization has set for itself. A budget answers several basic questions:

1. What will it cost to do what we want to do?
2. From what sources will revenues come?

3. How will revenues be allocated?
4. What will it cost to do each of the activities we want to do?

The organization's yearly plan, expressed in dollars, is one of the many tools managers use to measure monthly progress toward the organization's goals. The budget can be broken down into twelve monthly budgets that show projected expenses and revenues. An itemized monthly report can show on which items the manager is overspending or underspending and whether or not the revenue projections are being met (or even exceeded) for each month. This information allows a manager to judge whether changes may be required before the end of the year so that he will neither overspend nor underspend his budget.

As we shall see, the budget is at the core of a manager's responsibility in that it is an important way of expressing the program's inputs, throughputs, and outputs (discussed in Chapter 2). As such, the degree of control a program manager is allowed to have over changes in the budget reflects the extent of his authority to guide and use the resources being devoted to his program. Consequently, he must be thoroughly familiar with every part of the budget so that he can exercise his responsibility, be accountable to top management, and interpret the vagaries of the budget to subordinates.

THE BUDGET CYCLE

Since budgets are plans, it would seem to make sense that they should be developed only once a year. In theory, and often in practice, that is the way budgeting is done. (Some jurisdictions, the state of Florida, for example, are experimenting with biennial budgets.) Unfortunately, human services agencies must deal with several funding sources, each of which may have a different schedule for submitting budgets and different fiscal years. For example, the federal government begins its fiscal year on October 1 but many state governments begin the fiscal year on July 1. Moreover, some municipalities and county governments begin the fiscal year on January 1. Budget plans take effect at the beginning of the fiscal year. Therefore, the start of the fiscal year of a particular agency will be dictated by the start of the fiscal year of its major funding source but must take into account the financial schedules of other funding sources as well. Most middle managers, however, usually need to worry about only one fiscal year—that of the parent agency.

A budget cycle structures the development and execution of a budget. It is a schedule of events that begins with a notification from the agency's chief executive officer that program or departmental budget estimates must be formulated and ends with a year-end evaluation of the resulting program (Lee and Johnson, 1977). The specific parts of the budget cycle vary from agency to agency and from one funding jurisdiction to another. The parts of the budget cycle discussed in this section, although they may have different labels from place to place, are fairly common.

The first part of the cycle is the "call for estimates." Usually three to four months before the beginning of the fiscal year the chief executive officer of an agency sends a memorandum to each program manager or department head asking them to prepare estimates of income and expenses for the following fiscal year. He will also usually give the managers guidelines for preparing the budget in terms of what forms to use and when estimates are due. He may also give the managers information about the expected income of the entire agency from funding sources and about the service priorities of the agency, as well as the priorities of its major funding sources. This information will help the manager know what aspects of his program should be given more emphasis—expressed as financial resources—and what limitations he has in planning his program's budget.

In order to prepare such estimates the program manager must begin the second phase of the cycle which we shall call "planning and goal setting." During this phase the manager develops a specific plan for the coming fiscal year. This plan is expressed as a series of goals with specific objectives that can be measured. For example, it is not enough to state the following as a goal: "This program will provide outpatient mental health services to children." Such an objective is too vague and cannot be measured. A measurable goal would be: "This program will deliver 2,000 units (1 unit = 90 minutes) of outpatient mental health therapy to children between the ages of 0 and 18 years." Such a statement makes clear what service will be offered, the way the service will be measured, and the population that will receive the service. Program goals for existing services should reflect the manager's knowledge of his program's track record for the previous year and the current year. It should take into account changes in the program's orientation and changes in his staff's capabilities in terms of the quantity and the quality of their work. As we saw in the previous chapter, the best planning efforts are those that involve the entire staff so that the work group will be more highly motivated to meet the goals that are set.

Once goals have been set the manager enters the third phase, "establishing costs and revenues," wherein he prepares a tentative budget. Every cost of a program must be identified and listed. Personnel costs will usually be higher than any other cost item—usually between 60 and 80 percent of the total program budget. Other direct costs of the program, overhead costs, and capital expenses (the cost of nonconsumable equipment, usually over $100) must also be estimated. (The difference between direct and indirect expenses will be discussed later in this chapter.)

Just as a family cannot live beyond its means by continually being overdrawn on its checking account, a program cannot plan to spend more than it can earn as revenue; revenues must equal costs. Revenue for human services programs generally comes from three major sources. The most important source for most programs is a variety of federal, state, and local government grants. Another source is fees for services, including third party insurance, purchase of service funds, and cash fees from clients. The third source of revenue is contracts with other public and private organizations for particular services. For example, a business or industry may contract with a community mental health center to provide preemployment psychological screening for its top executives. Costs and revenue will be discussed further in the following section when the details of preparing a budget are reviewed.

After costs and revenues have been estimated and listed on the appropriate forms, the budget is ready for the next phase of the cycle, "submission to the chief executive officer." The budgets of the various programs of an agency are prepared by the program manager and are then aggregated as a total budget for the whole agency. It is the responsibility of the chief executive of the agency to put this budget together with the needs, goals, and financial condition of the entire agency in mind. In most agencies each program manager has an opportunity to meet with the executive, along with the agency's business manager, to answer questions about his budget proposal. The manager must be prepared with an impressive presentation of past accomplishments and plans for the future in order to defend his proposal for continued or increased funding. But bear in mind that a variety of factors determines whether the executive will modify or eliminate parts of some program proposals.

In the event that agencywide limitations in funding require budget cuts in certain programs, managers would do well to set priorities in their own programs so that they can suggest areas for cuts to the chief executive. This will give the chief executive more options and allow the managers the choice of how and where to modify their programs.

"Board approval" is sought when the total agency budget is complete. The chief executive officer submits the budget to the board of directors, usually through its finance committee, for approval. Boards of directors of nonprofit human services agencies bear the final responsibility for the agency's budget. They must carefully consider the budgetary plan in terms of the agency's primary mission and in terms of whether or not projected revenues meet projected costs. They also must decide whether or not these projections are reasonable within the context of what they know about the agency's productivity record and the ability of the agency to attract revenue. It is possible at this phase of the budget cycle that the board may require cuts in certain items of the budget, thus requiring program managers and the executive to go back to the drawing board to develop a revised budget. The revised budget will be sent to the board for its approval.

Board approval of the budget is not, as some might expect, the end of the annual budget cycle. Since the budget is a plan of action for the year, the budget cycle must include a mechanism to determine, on an ongoing basis, whether or not the plan is being effectively carried out. This mechanism is called "program evaluation" or a "program audit" (Lee and Johnson, 1977). Program evaluators and accountants employed by the agency generally are resources who program managers and top management must use throughout the year to insure that program goals are being met and that expenditures are not exceeding revenue. At the end of a fiscal year, independent fiscal auditors are employed by the board of directors to make sure that funds were properly accounted for and spent. Funding agencies may also send their own auditors to the agency to examine how funds were used. Although none of us very much enjoys having other people scrutinizing our work, it is important to remember that this phase of the budget cycle is a vital part of the feedback mechanism for the system (discussed in Chapter 2). Without continual feedback all systems tend to stray from their original goals and in the human services this means that clients are not served in the manner they should be served (this subject is covered in more detail in Chapter 9).

PREPARING A BUDGET: A CASE STUDY

In order to understand the basic elements of program budgeting, which is the crux of financial management for a program manager, we shall examine a hypothetical program's budget development through the first four phases of the budget cycle. The budget submission phase and the board approval phase will not be discussed because once the manager has gone through the first four phases of the budget cycle, the budget is essentially out of his hands.

Let us consider a day treatment program in a community mental health center. The budget will be kept artificially simple and the program will be discussed in a general way to make it similar to small programs in a variety of human services agencies. Let us assume that the fiscal year of the program's parent agency begins on July 1.

On March 1 the executive director sends a memorandum to all program managers that starts the year's budget cycle. The call for estimates informs all the managers that the agency's business manager, board finance committee, and executive director have determined that the outlook for the coming fiscal year is not good in terms of increases in monies from federal and state sources, its two major sources of funding. On the other hand, the director writes, the agency fully expects to maintain its *current* level of funding and expects each program to make greater efforts to generate revenue from insurance and other private sources by increasing productivity. In his memorandum the director also indicates that the agency's internal program priorities for the coming year are the elderly, chronic patients, and young children of severely emotionally disturbed parents. The format for the budget estimates is presented in the memo and the date for submission of program budgets to him is set at May 1.

At the next staff meeting of the day treatment program the manager informs the staff of two paraprofessionals and a secretary that it is time to prepare next year's budget. He explains the director's budget message and asks them to begin thinking about a response. He points out that their program serves two of the three priority populations, elderly and chronic clients. He suggests that the director and the board of directors may be willing to put more resources into the day program because they serve a priority population even though the total agency budget will probably remain the same next year as it is for the current year. This would mean that other services of the total agency would have to be cut in order to allow for an increase in the day treatment program budget, but that is the director's problem, not the manager's.

The staff and the manager agree that an increase for the day treatment program should be proposed, but opinions vary as to how much. Expensive equipment, new staff positions, and big raises for existing staff are advocated. The manager suggests that everyone think about these options until the next meeting. In the meantime, he promises to look at the program's costs and productivity for the current year so that the data to justify budget increases will be available. By the time the staff meeting has ended, the planning and goal setting phase of the budget cycle has been launched with everyone committed to making suggestions for next year's program at the following meeting.

By the time of the next meeting the manager has done his homework. He announces that as of February, the program is right on target for its productivity goal of 5,300 units of service for the year (for the day treatment program, a unit of service is defined as a four-hour block of time spent in the program by one client). The program has so far generated 3,600 units, averaging 450 units of service per month. They will have no trouble reaching their goal if productivity stays about the same for the rest of the year (i.e., $450 \times 12 = 5,400$, or 100 units over the goal). The manager also announces that he has spoken with the executive director, who is pleased with the day program and, in view of its service to priority populations, encouraged the manager to increase the program's productivity in the coming year. This implies an increase in costs. After talking with the business manager, the program evaluator, the chairperson of the finance committee, and other prgram managers, the manager estimates that roughly a 20 to 30 percent increase in productivity would be reasonable given the increased demand for day treatment services. A discussion of this information ensues and staff members agree that it is clear that an increase in productivity would bring an increase in budgeted resources. Since more equipment would not necessarily affect an increase in productivity or quality, everyone agrees that the productivity increase can be achieved through the addition of a paraprofessional. The manager thanks the staff for their suggestions and tells them that he will show them the budget proposal before it is submitted to the director.

The manager decides to increase the productivity goal by a third since he will have three instead of two clinical staff members if his proposal is accepted. Therefore, he sets the productivity goal for the following year at 8,000 units of service. He also plans to have the program offer the same kinds of services that it currently provides. This decision, based on a careful assessment of needs in the community, ends the planning and goal setting phase. The manager must now determine the actual cost of his program for the coming year.

In determining the cost of a program the manager must consider both direct and indirect costs. "Direct costs" are expenses directly associated with the production of units of service; for example, staff salaries, consultant fees, supplies used for treatment activities, and rent. "Indirect costs" cannot be identified with any particular unit of productivity or direct service but are support costs necessary for the functioning of the entire agency; for example, the costs of the organization's personnel department, business office, client records department, and administrative office. These costs are allocated to the service providing programs in such a way that the programs share indirect costs proportional to each program's size and the extent to which each benefits from the services of the supportive programs or departments. There are numerous bases for allocating indirect costs to each program. A few examples are:

Personnel Department—based on number of employees in each program.

Client Records—based on percentage of records maintained for each program.

Program Evaluation—based on number of studies done for each program or amount of time spent on each program.

Business Office—based on number of bills generated by each program.

Indirect costs are usually assigned to programs by top administration. The manager will not have to estimate indirect costs but should understand how they are arrived at so that he can influence their allocation in a manner that favors his own program and explain how they are determined to his subordinates.

Getting back to our example, the manager of the day treatment program employs historical data to estimate the direct costs of various items to be used by his program in the coming year. In essentially the same manner that he set the productivity goal for the coming year, he first determines the direct costs of the current year. He does this by looking at monthly reports for the current year and figuring the average costs *per month* of each cost item. He projects the year-end cost of each category by multiplying the average monthly cost by twelve. He determines that the direct year-end cost of his program will be $57,252. Table 7-1 breaks down the costs by line item expense category.

The indirect, or allocated, costs of the program are also indicated in Table 7-1. These costs, also called overhead, are, as we saw above, usually set by the executive director based upon the extent to which the program makes use of the services of support departments. The day treatment program will be allocated approximately $4,020 of indirect costs for the current year. Therefore, the total projected year-end cost of the day treatment program is $61,272. Since productivity for the current year is nearly exactly what had been predicted, let us assume that the projected year-end cost of the program is exactly what was budgeted for the year.

Now the manager has the two pieces of information needed to plan the program's costs for the coming year: projected year-end costs for the current year and an idea of what increases will be requested for the coming year. All he has to do to determine the cost for the coming year is add these two figures. Table 7-2 shows that with the addition of a new position, 5 percent merit raises for existing staff, and a one-third increase in supplies and allocated costs, the cost of the day treatment program for the coming year will be $80,000.

The manager's next task in preparing the budget proposal is to estimate the program's revenues for the coming year. His guide in estimating revenue for the coming year is of course the projected cost since revenue *must* equal cost in nonprofit organizations. It is certainly acceptable for a program's revenue during any given year to exceed costs. But in preparing a budget a manager must be assured that revenue will at least meet his costs. The point during the year at which revenue catches up to program costs is called the

TABLE 7-1. Projected Year-End Costs for Current Year

	Costs Through February	Average Cost per Month	Projected Annual Cost	
Personnel*	$33,296	$4,162	$49,944	
Rent†	2,672	334	4,008	
Supplies	2,200	275	3,300	
	38,168	4,771	$57,252	projected year-end direct cost
Allocated	2,680††	335	$ 4,020	projected year-end indirect cost
TOTAL			$61,272	

*Includes salaries plus 16 percent for FICA and benefits.
†Includes utilities, telephone, and insurance as well as office space.
††Estimated by business manager based on a cost allocation study done at midyear.

TABLE 7-2. Day Treatment Program Costs for Current Year and Next Fiscal Year

	Current Year	Proposed for Next Year	Explanation
Personnel			
Manager	$15,200	$16,000	5% raise
2 Paraprofessionals	20,260	32,000	5% raise; one additional position
1 Secretary	7,600	8,000	5% raise
	43,060	56,000	
FICA and Benefits	6,884	8,960	16% of total personnel
	49,944	64,960	costs
Rent and Utilities	4,008	4,608	8% increase for inflation
Supplies	3,300	4,400	33.3% increase for inflation and for supplies for new worker.
Allocated Costs	4,020	6,032	
TOTALS	$61,272	$80,000	

"break-even point." Any revenue above the break-even point is surplus, which in a nonprofit organization is used to make up for deficits in other programs or to increase services in the agency.

In estimating revenue it is necessary to determine the program's rate. The "rate" is the amount of money that is ordinarily charged for each unit of service; it is the "advertised" price of the unit. The rate per unit should at least equal the cost per unit of service. The following simple equation shows how to determine the unit cost:

$$\frac{\text{total program cost}}{\text{volume}} = \text{cost per unit} = \text{rate}$$

The equation for the day treatment program unit cost and rate for the coming year (where volume represents units of service) would be:

$$\frac{\$80,000}{8,000} = \$10$$

The rate is needed to determine insurance fees and other private fees. It is also necessary to determine the rate when government funding is directly related to the unit cost or to the actual number of service units delivered through purchase of service contracts.

By far the largest category of revenue in human services organizations is grants. Grants can be from private foundations, agencies such as the United

Way, or federal, state, and local governments. Grants are most often awarded to an agency in a lump sum and allocated to programs within the agency by the executive director. It is therefore necessary for the manager in our example to confer with the director to get as much information as possible about how much revenue from each source of grants can reasonably be expected for the day treatment program. Using this discussion and discussions with the program evaluator and the business manager regarding estimated revenue from fees for service, the manager develops the revenue budget estimate shown in Table 7-3.

Since federal mental health program priorities match the agency's program priorities, the manager projects his largest increase in revenues from the federal operations grant. He decides to ask for the same amount of state funding even though the state's priorities are in areas not addressed by the day treatment program. On the advice of the executive director he projects a substantial increase in revenue from county funds. Finally, the projected revenue from fees for service is increased by more than one-third to keep pace with inflation and to cover the cost of an additional staff member.

The day treatment program's budget proposal is now ready to be submitted to the executive director. But first the manager carefully explains the proposal to his staff so that they fully understand it. He stresses the relationship between hiring a new staff member, which everyone heartily endorses, and the increase in projected units of service for the coming year. All staff members support the manager's budget proposal and ask to be kept informed of its progress during the remaining phases of the budget cycle.

The budget is submitted to the executive director a few days before the May 1 due date. Since the manager diligently conferred with a variety of resource people in the agency while preparing the proposal, including the director himself, the day treatment program's budget is proclaimed by the director to be in good order and just about what he had in mind. With only minor modifications in the revenue sources, the budget is sent along to the finance committee of the board of directors with the budget proposals of all the other programs in the agency. The board approves the budget and it is implemented beginning on July 1.

TABLE 7-3. **Revenue by Source for Current Year and Next Fiscal Year**

	CURRENT YEAR	PROPOSED FOR NEXT YEAR
Federal Operations Grant	$30,275	$40,000
State Mental Health Funds	20,000	20,000
County Funds	2,000	5,000
Fees	9,000	15,000
TOTALS	$61,275	$80,000

Although many parts of the budget preparation process have been abbreviated in the above discussion, the basic components of any program budget have been highlighted. The actual procedure and the exact budget categories and dollar amounts will vary from program to program and from one agency to another. But the beginning middle manager in the human services, with these fundamental concepts in mind, should be able to master the budget process with a little practice. For additional information on budgeting and the preparation of budgets, the new manager should review the following sources: Demone and Harshbarger (1973); Feldman (1973); Lee and Johnson (1977); Matthews (1977); Smith (1977); and Sweeny and Wisner (1975).

MONITORING AND CONTROL

While the preparation of a budget is usually an annual project, operating within budgetary constraints is a day-to-day task for the manager. A manager who regularly overspends his budget each month is like the person who writes checks for more than the balance in his account several days before depositing his biweekly paycheck. Conversely, if he is too cautious about spending, the manager may not be using all the resources available to him to the best advantage of his program. In order to avoid spending too much or too little of the budget in any given month the manager must monitor his program's expenditures and control the flow of money in and out of his program.

A budget is a statement of a program's most basic intentions (Sweeny and Wisner, 1975). It addresses a number of questions: What do we plan to do? What will it cost to accomplish our goals? How shall we recover these costs? The answers to these questions are intentions and are expressed in the annual budget, where costs are related to program plans and provisions are made for revenue. This annual statement of intentions can be divided into twelve monthly budgets further divided into categories of expenditure (such as rent, salaries, and supplies) and revenue. By examining a monthly statement of intentions, or plans for spending and revenue, a manager knows the exact amount of money allotted for each category for each month. Such a monthly statement is called a "budget report." Table 7–4 is an example of a monthly budget report.

What other information does a budget report contain? It indicates what actually was spent in each budget category for each month. Whereas the statement of intention (budget) says what we planned to do, the statement of action (actual) says what we really did. For example, the line for supplies for the month of April indicates the program planned to spend $275 in that category for that month. However, in another column the report shows that the program actually spent $305, or $30 more than was budgeted. The third

TABLE 7-4. **Monthly Budget Report of Expenses and Revenues for April**

	CURRENT MONTH			YEAR TO DATE		
Costs	*Budget*	*Actual*	*Under/ (Over)*	*Budget*	*Actual*	*Under/ (Over)*
Personnel	$4,162	$3,980	$ 182	$49,944	$42,625	$ 7,319
Rent	334	334		4,008	3,674	334
Supplies	275	305	(30)	3,000	4,331	(1,331)
Allocated	335	335		4,020	5,960	(1,940)
	$5,106	$4,954	$ 152	$60,972	$56,590	$ 4,382
Revenues	*Budget*	*Actual*	*Under/ (Over)*	*Budget*	*Actual*	*Under/ (Over)*
Federal Operations Grant	$2,700	$2,700		$27,000	$27,000	
State Mental Health Funds	1,500	1,500		15,000	15,000	
County Funds	600	600		6,000	4,000	2,000
Fees	1,206	897	309	12,060	14,003	(1,943)
	$6,097	$5,697	$309	$60,972	$60,003	$ 57

column shows the difference between what was budgeted and what was actually spent. The bottom line of the expense part of the report indicates whether or not the total expenditures exceed the total revenues, which are also shown. The report shows what was budgeted, what actually was spent, what was earned, and the deviation from the budget for the prior month and for the year to date.

The monthly budget report is an important tool for program managers in that the information it contains helps him determine whether or not mid-year changes in plans for expenditures and/or revenue need to be made. The manager must decide whether the variance is good news or bad news (generally, if actual exceeds budget, the news is bad). He must determine what went wrong for the month or for the year to date. He must examine whether or not the budget plan was overoptimistic or flawed in other ways. Furthermore, he must determine whether productivity is too low and why, if it is. Or, he must see whether certain costs have risen in response to inflation or other factors that were not planned for when the budget was prepared.

When significant variations between the budget column and the actual column begin to show up, the manager should start thinking about the points listed above. He should also consult with other staff and the business manager on how to interpret the variations. Ultimately, though, if the variance continues to increase, the manager must take action. The action taken will depend upon the nature of the problem with the budget. Generally, there are two basic actions a manager can take if he finds that he is consistently overspending his budget. First, expenses can be held down by curtailing the purchase of supplies or other items or, in extreme situations, laying off personnel (see Chapter 10). Second, one can increase revenue by increasing the rate charged to clients sufficiently to match the cost or by increasing productivity if there is a fee for service contract in effect. Obviously, a third action is to hold down costs *and* to increase revenue. Of course, if the program serves only nonpaying, indigent clients and does not operate under a purchase of service contract with a funding agency, an increase in productivity will not increase revenues.

Note that the prospect of increasing fees for services poses a dilemma for the human services manager. On the one hand he may face a serious curtailment in the quantity of services offered if he cannot increase fees in order to pay salaries and other expenses. On the other hand, higher fees may drive away indigent and even middle-class clients who desperately need the service. Under these circumstances the manager must develop a compromise that maximizes revenues while driving as few people as possible away from the program.

The manager who fails to use the monthly budget report as a tool to monitor and control his program's expenditures and revenues will eventually have his freedom to act taken from him. If the variance between intentions and action becomes intolerable, top management will step in and take control of the situation. When top administrators are compelled to intervene the problem usually has reached the point at which the remedy is more drastic than it would have been at an earlier stage.

We shall now turn our attention to the manager's authority and the motivation of subordinates as a way of discussing how managers get things done in their organizations.

REFERENCES

DEMONE, H. W., AND HARSHBARGER, D. *The Planning and Administration of Human Services*. New York: Behavioral Publications, 1973.

FELDMAN, S. "Budgeting and behavior." In S. Feldman (ed.), *The Administration of Mental Health Services*. Springfield: Charles C Thomas, 1973.

LEE, R. D., AND JOHNSON, R. W. *Public Budgeting Systems*. 2d edition. Baltimore: University Park Press, 1977.

MATTHEWS, L. M. *Practical Operating Budgeting*. New York: McGraw-Hill, 1977.

SMITH, T. S. "Budgeting subsystems." In W. A. Hargreaves, C. C. Attkisson, and J. E. Sorensen (eds.), *Resource Materials for Community Mental Health Evaluation*. Rockville: National Institute of Mental Health, 1977.

SWEENY, A., AND WISNER, J.N. *Budgeting Fundamentals for Nonfinancial Executives*. New York: Amacom, 1975.

Getting Things Done

The ultimate proof of a successful manager is that he gets things done. Our discussions of planning and budgeting, communication, and organizational behavior notwithstanding, the real emphasis is, or should be, on end results—the delivery of high quality, effective services as efficiently as possible. Elegant plans mean very little if the manager cannot marshal the staff to *achieve* the quantitative and qualitative goals of the program. From what we know of human nature and human behavior, it takes something other than cracking the whip to get things done. But it takes more than being a perpetual nice guy, too. In this discussion of how a manager gets things done, we shall examine a potpourri of management concepts.

Why a potpourri? Why not a few simple, specific concepts that will guide managers in accomplishing organizational goals? The best reason is that the field of managing for results is diverse. Issues related to accomplishing organizational goals—power and authority, worker motivation and productivity, special management techniques, and the place of the human services professional in a bureaucracy—will be covered briefly in this chapter. But what of the host of other problems that confront a manager who is attempting to manage for results? What of interdisciplinary conflicts, political constraints, competing staff expectations? And what of the constant lack of funds?

These real-life questions must be dealt with by managers. The following sections will attempt to address some of these issues, albeit indirectly. Direct answers must come from each manager's experience with the multitude of intraorganizational problems and from the manager's personal and organizational resources for dealing with these problems. Such solutions must satisfy workers *and* accomplish the organization's goals. To help him in this task, the manager should keep in mind certain aspects of organizational life. One is the value of a positive attitude that is conveyed to all members of the organization. A positive attitude is fostered by a sense of humor, enthusiasm for programmatic goals, and unwillingness to get bogged down in the pettiness and negativism of chronic complainers.

A very important aspect of organizational life that a manager should keep in mind revolves around the question of why people work. This subject will be discussed later in this chapter and in Chapter 10. Nonetheless, it is crucial to remember that human services professionals want more from work than a paycheck. They want opportunities for career development and advancement and intellectual and emotional stimulation at work. A manager must strive to discover the superordinate goals of each subordinate and continually search for ways those goals can be met within the context of the organization and *its* goals.

Finally, before moving on to the question of control, power, and authority, let us pause to consider the manager's responsibility to foster friendly competition among subordinates and between his program and others in the agency. Such friendly competition creates an air of excitement and makes work fun. The manager, however, must beware of setting up common enemies outside the program as a rallying point and of encouraging angry and destructive competition among employees. Just as the friendly side of competition can foster a sense of excitement that can be harnessed toward the accomplishment of organizational goals, the unfriendly side can subvert organizational goals and keep everyone from getting things done in behalf of the program's clients.

CONTROL, AUTHORITY, AND POWER

In discussions about management and in the management literature one often runs across the terms "control" and the "control function of management." The word "control" in this context refers to the manager's responsibility to regulate and direct the work of his organization. It is not used to connote domination of one person by another. In exercising the control function, a manager first establishes certain performance standards and communicates them to subordinates. He then measures actual performance at regular intervals. Finally, the manager takes corrective action if performance lags behind goals. He may reexamine the goals to determine whether they are realistic. Or, he may decide that the goals are realistic and that workers must be prodded, encouraged, or given incentives to produce more work. The manager may also give directives to subordinates to change or modify their behavior regarding the performance of certain tasks.

A manager's ability to exercise the control function depends on three factors. The first, which will be dealt with more fully in the next chapter, is the information available about the performance of the work group. The manager must have accurate and timely measures of the results of subordinates' efforts. The other two things that determine a manager's ability to exercise control are authority and power. These two concepts are usually emotionally charged—most often negatively—in human services organizations and warrant closer examination.

Authority and power: what's the difference? Authority is the right to make decisions about something. It is historically based on ownership or property rights. For example, only you have the authority to decide who shall drive your car or, in most instances, who shall enter your home. One who owns something also owns the right—has the authority—to make decisions pertaining to that thing. In organizations, ownership belongs to the board of directors; they have the ultimate right to make decisions about the organization. They also have ultimate responsibility for decisions they have delegated to the executive director and his subordinates. The board of directors delegates the authority to make some decisions to the executive director, who in turn delegates some authority downward in the organization. In this way, authority, and the accompanying responsibility, are shared, with ultimate responsibility at the top of the organizational hierarchy. It is important for everyone in the organization to understand who has authority for certain decisions. As Winston Churchill is supposed to have suggested, no good can ever come from making "a number one move from a number two position."

Power is quite different from authority. Everyone who has authority has power, but everyone who has power does not necessarily have authority. Power is the possession of influence over others; it takes many forms and is rarely absolute in organizations. French and Raven (1960) delineated five basic types of power:

1. *Reward power*—the ability to satisfy the needs and wants of others through rewards.
2. *Coercive power*—influence based upon fear of punishment or retaliation.
3. *Legitimate power*—power based on authority.
4. *Referent power*—power based upon one's personal attraction or charisma.
5. *Expert power*—power based upon knowledge or special expertise.

All of these types of power can be a part of the repertoire of managers and each can be used depending upon the internal environment of the organization at any particular time. A beginning manager in the human services must develop a style for using power in the most effective way. Power, like leadership, depends heavily upon subordinates and their interactions with the manager. This means that certain power strategies work best in certain types of situation. For example, expert power is necessary for a psychotherapy group leader to facilitate a group; whereas legitimate power is necessary for that person's supervisor to insist that he handle his paperwork for the therapy group in a more organized and timely manner.

Perhaps the most troublesome thing about power is knowing that you have it and understanding that other people know you have it. Subordinates treat those who have power over them differently from the way they treat each other. A manager whose identity is that of a clinician will have a good deal of difficulty getting used to the fact that he has, and is perceived to have, power over others. It takes time to make such a transition in one's view of oneself. A new manager who denies that he has power, who says and thinks, "I'm one of you," merely prolongs the period of adjustment not only to his power but to his role as a manager, too.

There is a misconception in the human services that power and authority are so easily abused that they must be inherently evil. Most individuals have had their share of unpleasant experiences with tyrants who delight in their power or with superiors who are so uncomfortable with their power that they apply it inconsistently. Perhaps our views of power are to a great extent shaped by these unpleasant experiences. But our knowledge of our world tells us that biological, mechanical, and social systems cannot function properly without a regulator. Consider an amoeba without a nucleus, a speeding jet without a pilot, or a country without a president or prime minister. The question that new human services managers must struggle with is not whether they will *have* authority and power but *how* will they exercise it. Albert Camus, in a notebook entry for June 1938, expressed their dilemma magnificently: "It is difficult to realize that one can be superior to a large number of people without thereby becoming someone superior. And in that lies his genuine superiority" (Camus, 1963, p. 94).

SOME IDEAS ABOUT PRODUCTIVITY

Productivity in human services can be defined as the transformation of professional and paraprofessional skills and efforts into services for clients. To return to the systems model in Chapter 2, staff knowledge and skills constitute input, the efforts and skills of staff interacting with clients constitute throughput, or process, and the services that result and the benefits that accrue to the clients constitute output. "Productivity" is an umbrella term for this entire system. Productivity may be expressed as a simple equation:

$$\frac{\text{output}}{\text{input}} = \text{productivity index}$$

Productivity is tied to the livelihood of the organization in two important ways. The first concerns the core purpose of the organization. Human services organizations exist to produce services for people. To the extent that human services agencies do not make it their primary business to produce services, they experience the effects of entropy and begin to lose their identity. When this begins to happen, all of the organization's constituencies—clients, staff, funding sources, board of directors—lose interest and decrease their efforts in behalf of the agency. When this chain of events starts, the existence of the agency is threatened. But, like an ancient oak tree, agencies take a long time to die. In the meantime, dying agencies become rigid and unchanging; staff morale and the quality of services to clients are severely diminished.

Funding is the second important way that productivity is tied to the livelihood of an organization. In these days of public accountability, agencies that do not produce services cannot expect to be funded; production of services is inextricably tied to revenue. An organization's ability to collect private and insurance fees and government purchase of service funds sufficient to meet all its operating expenses is dependent upon its ability to deliver services to clients.

In managing productivity a manager has several tasks. Although he may involve the staff in this undertaking, the responsibility is his alone. The first task is to determine the production capacity of the work group. This step was briefly discussed in the chapter on budgeting. The manager must make determinations about how many units of service can be provided given the available staff hours. It is necessary to allow for vacations, sick time, staff turnover, client cancellations, holidays, and other factors in making this determination. Nonetheless, it is equally important to explore and invalidate the myths about why more "simply can't be done." Are staff *really* overworked or do they think they are? What organizational and motivational factors are limiting their production capacity? For example, if office space is a limiting factor, why can't offices, clients, and professionals be scheduled differently so as to maximize available space?

Once the work group's capacity for productivity has been established, the manager's next task is to communicate expectations to the staff in the clearest manner possible. This is best done in staff meetings and in writing. Also, it is well continually to remind workers what productivity standards are for the current time period (a month or a year) and that these standards are subject to modification at a later date. The manager's other tasks regarding productivity concern incentives, rewards, and control. They are discussed elsewhere in this chapter.

An agency often becomes concerned with productivity only when problems arise, such as diminished government funding, which causes the agency to rely on private and insurance fees or when new payment mechanisms are adopted (e.g., state purchase of service contracts). But productivity should be a constant concern of managers because pressure from funding sources to be productive is likely to be applied at any time. We shall discuss management techniques to assist productivity in the next section. The manager can do many simple things to let the staff know where the organization stands in meeting its goals and to encourage productivity. A middle manager in an outpatient clinic once drew a six-foot-high thermometer with the year's goal for units of service at the top. The thermometer was calibrated into months, with the cumulative year-to-date units of service goal at each month. Various encouragements and humorous urgings to produce more services were written on the thermometer such as "We can do it!" and "They said it couldn't be done!" Excitement ran high at the end of every month as the staff watched the red paint rise closer and closer to the goal. In fact, so much excitement was generated by this device that the agency's executive director was enticed to treat this program's entire staff to a day at the beach when their productivity exceeded the goal by several hundred units. This program increased its productivity from 72 percent of its year-to-date goal in October of the fiscal year to 104 percent in April.

A similar management tool is a monthly productivity report (see Table 8-1). Yearly goals are made before the start of the fiscal year and are expressed in units of service. The nature of the units of service will depend upon the type of service offered by the program. A unit could be an hour of counseling, placement of a child for adoption, or a bed occupied by a patient in a hospital for one day. The yearly goal is then divided into monthly goals. The simplest way is to divide the yearly goal by twelve. Another, more complicated way is to project different monthly goals based on the program's previous experience with busy and slow seasons. The report should have a row for the number of units expected to be delivered each month, the actual number delivered, the cumulative number for the year to date, and the percentage of the year-to-date goal that has been achieved. This monitoring device will allow the manager to regulate the efforts of the staff to meet deficiencies on a monthly basis. The report should be shared with the staff to make them aware of their progress and so that an esprit de corps can develop. Some agencies use monthly productivity reports for each staff member. This approach, however, can foster destructive intraprogram competition; competition may have some short-term benefits, but in the long run productivity may suffer with this method.

Another aspect of productivity, especially relevant in the human services, is the quality of the product. In the struggle to generate revenue, quantitative goals can overshadow qualitative goals so that a program is producing a high number of units of a mediocre or poor quality service. This can happen even when the absolute number of units is held to a reasonable level but the number of clients served is excessive. For example, a counseling agency with a large waiting list began seeing clients for counseling once every three or four weeks. The waiting list was rapidly diminished, but many clients began missing their appointments and measures of counseling effectiveness began to decline. Moreover, counselors' caseloads became so

TABLE 8-1. Outpatient Monthly Report for April

	July	Aug.	Sept.	Oct.	Nov.	Dec.	Jan.	Feb.	Mar.	Apr.	May	June	Totals
Actual Units of Service	562	495	522	642	597	547	938	895	1036	798			
Actual Year to Date	562	1057	1579	2221	2818	3365	4303	5198	6234	7032			
Goal Year to Date	675	1350	2025	2700	3375	4050	4725	5400	6075	6750	7425	8100	8100 Staff Hours
Percent Goal Year to Date	83	78	78	82	83	83	91	96	103	104			
Total Visits	560	632	716	974	875	675	1214	1006	1229	951			

large that they could not keep track of what was going on with each client. The client recordkeeping also became overwhelming. The solution to this problem was for the manager to limit the number of open cases counselors could have, develop better screening techniques in order to decide who would be seen and who would not be seen, and develop methods of referring those who would not be seen to other agencies.

Quality care must be insured. This topic will be discussed in the next chapter. However, it is important to note that quality service is as much the manager's responsibility as is the amount of service rendered. In addition to procedural interventions in poor quality situations, in-service training can help staff develop skills in areas where their deficits may be affecting quality. In any case, a manager must always counterbalance concern for numbers of service units with concern for quality.

MOTIVATION

Motivation can be defined as the internal and external factors that determine the energy, willingness, and enthusiasm a person puts into any given task. What impels a person to do a job? To answer this question one must know in a general sense what that person's needs are and how he perceives his world.

People *need* many things to be satisfied and happy. Needs fall into two broad categories: physical and social-psychological. Physical needs are obvious. Social-psychological needs are more complex and elusive. It seems that once one need is satisfied, a person perceives something else that is necessary to his happiness. Hemingway expressed this point quite well in *Across the River and into the Trees* when he wrote, "Happiness, as you know, is a movable feast." Maslow (1954) based his well-known "hierarchy of needs" on this notion. Maslow theorized that people have needs that range from the basic needs of physical survival to the sense of becoming all that one is possible of achieving. His hierarchy begins with physiological needs and ascends through safety needs, belongingness or love needs, and esteem and status needs, to the need for self-actualization. Maslow's theory, although not entirely supported by research (Filley, House, and Kerr, 1976), has a great deal of popular appeal. It suggests that a manager who attempts to meet a worker's needs at the lower half of the hierarchy may be doing little to motivate the worker if his needs are for recognition or self-actualization. This may be why higher salaries are often only a temporary motivator: although everyone would like to be paid more for his work, a pay raise will not necessarily help a person feel self-actualized. Human relations theory, discussed in Chapter 2, and Herzberg, Mausner, and Snyderman's "two-factor theory" (1959) also rely heavily on the needs people have. They consider economic security, the desire to be creative, the need for recognition and advancement, and a sense of performing interesting and important work to be important in motivating people to work.

Two other theories of worker motivation have received considerably more support through research. The first of these is called "value expectancy theory." First stated by Lewin (1951) and expanded by Vroom (1964) the theory specifies:

> People expect different outcomes or consequences from different courses of action and prefer certain outcomes over others.
> People are motivated when they believe that their own actions will have a good chance of bringing about outcomes they prefer.

A person will be highly motivated to work is he has good reason to believe that his diligent work today will result in a promotion later or in some other desired reward. Conversely, if a worker believes that his attempts to be promoted will prove futile, he will not be motivated to work hard. The implications for managers are quite clear. Managers must be prepared to deliver promised rewards so that workers will believe that their efforts will be rewarded. False promises will disincline workers to do any more than that which is required to keep their jobs.

"Inequity theory" is the second theory of motivation that has been supported by research (Filley, House, and Kerr, 1976). This theory suggests that when people perceive a difference between their own situation as compared to that of others in similar positions, there is tension both within the individuals involved and within the work group. This means, for example, that a person who feels he is underpaid will decrease his efforts so that they are commensurate with his pay. On the other hand, a person who feels overpaid will increase his efforts so that his level of work will match his level of pay. When there is a perceived balance between effort and reward, tension is reduced; people will continually strive to reduce tension to an optimal level. It is important to note that, the example above notwithstanding, this theory does not concern itself only with economic rewards but considers the entire range of rewards for work from money to recognition to advancement within the organization. It is the manager's responsibility to proffer rewards that will insure the highest level of motivation possible in his staff. Even when fiscal constraints make money rewards hard to come by, good managers can reward subordinates in a variety of ways if they are sensitive to each person's aspirations, physical and social-psychological wants and needs, and other reasons for working. For example, a worker can be rewarded with a flexible work schedule that would allow him to go back to school part-time.

Another way of approaching the question "What makes people work?" is to consider the work environment. Up to this point I have used the word "environment" chiefly to mean factors outside the organization that influence the total organization's behavior. In this context, however, environment refers to aspects of the organization itself that impinge on the individual's life at work.

Motivation to perform well is associated with a person's perception that there are opportunities for him within the organization. If opportunities are not there, motivation will be low and workers will quickly move on to jobs in other organizations that seem to offer more, not only financially, but in other ways, including challenge and advancement. Carlisle (1979) observed that "organizations tend to motivate the behavior they reward" (p. 274). He pointed out that good performance will not be a major concern of workers if the chief criterion for advancement is seniority. He added, "If being political and 'buttering up' the boss pays off, you will find more people trying to please such a supervisor's whims" (p. 275). Managers should be concerned not only with modifying individual behavior but with modifying the total work environment, too. The entire work environment should reward productivity and the achievement of *quality service* goals, not the preservation of a bureaucracy or the furthering of the selfish ends of a few people. Some of the ways that the work environment can be changed will be discussed in subsequent sections of this chapter.

The question of higher salaries as a motivator is often raised in discussions of motivation and productivity. There is certainly no doubt that people must be paid for work. (People committed to public service volunteerism are an obvious exception, but they are a minority). A salary that is perceived as fair makes people feel good about the effort they put forth. But, too much is often made of money as a motivator. People have, as we have seen, other needs that can be satisfied by their work. If these needs for recognition, opportunity, intellectual stimulation and challenge, and esteem are not being met, a raise in salary will be seen as a reward for only a short time. Soon the worker's life style will absorb the added money so that it will no longer be perceived as extra and the other, less tangible deficiencies in the job will still be present. Hofstede (1972) found in his research that in all but low income, minimal skill positions, money is an insignificant motivator. Equity theory tells us that if one person is paid less than another and is aware of the difference, money is a significant factor in his motivation. But, if people are fairly paid according to local standards of pay for similar positions and worker backgrounds, higher salaries will not, in the long run, solve an agency's motivation and productivity problems.

THREE APPROACHES TO PRODUCTIVITY

Management techniques come and go and new fads are constantly replacing old ones, just as new forms of psychotherapy seem to sweep the country with tiresome regularity. Some techniques, however, show more promise than others. We shall consider three popular management techniques that, despite some shortcomings, may yet prove to be durable ways to encourage and maintain productivity.

The first is "job enrichment." A legacy of scientific management and the rational-legal bureaucracy discussed in Chapter 2 is job specialization—everyone has a special task to perform and work is often excessively subdivided. The result is that coordination of efforts is complex (and may suffer) and workers become isolated, bored, and narrowminded. Job enrichment is really the opposite of specialization in that jobs are broadened in scope. For example, rather than assign a nurse on a medical-surgical ward the task of giving medications to all the patients on the ward while another nurse bathes the patients and another nurse writes progress notes and changes dressings, each nurse is assigned to two or three patients for whom she provides total care. Another example would be having social workers in a family services agency share the responsibility for intakes, counseling, family life education, and client follow-up instead of having different workers handle each separate task. As one can see from these two examples, job enrichment may have distinct benefits for clients, not the least of which is greater continuity of service. Benefits for the organization and the workers include less boredom, a more flexible staff, and the opportunity for each worker to explore and pursue a variety of interests and skills. These benefits for the worker, particularly the reduction of boredom, are associated with greater productivity.

There are certain disadvantages to job enrichment. Some workers feel that this technique changes a boring job into an exhausting one. Others prefer to develop proficiency in one particular task. Another potential disadvantage is that job enrichment may raise expectations that more pay for more broadly trained staff is or should be forthcoming. Dissatisfaction often results when these expectations cannot be met.

The second useful management technique is "management by objectives" (MBO). This term has been used by many people to mean many different things. Generally, though, there is agreement that MBO involves goal setting through consultation between a manager and each worker. The goals must be quantifiable and measurable. At the end of a specified period of time actual performance is compared to the original goals. The manager reviews progress, provides appropriate rewards, and modifies the original goals and identifies new ones as time goes on. For example, a manager and a physical therapist may jointly agree that the therapist will provide 450 two-hour physical therapy treatments in the coming year. The manager may also elect to set goals for the department as a whole by meeting with the entire staff and discussing productivity for the coming year. In either case, progress toward individual or departmental goals is monitored and appropriately rewarded each month. These clear, measurable goals can help everyone to monitor progress, and progress toward specific goals can by itself spur productivity. An additional advantage to MBO is that it is oriented toward the future and avoids conflicts about past deficiencies. MBO has the advantage of formalizing goal setting and monitoring rather than leaving this important managerial function to the whim of the manager.

MBO has many critics. Some say that the obsessive documentation and monitoring of goals and progress creates needless paperwork (Filley, House, and Kerr, 1976). Levinson (1970) argued that the goals are often those of management while the personal goals of individual workers are not fully considered. Also, managers may fail to coordinate their programs with those of other managers if attention to program goals becomes too narrowly focused. Finally, because of the difficulty of measuring certain kinds of goals, only the most easily measured objectives may be identified.

The third technique in modern management that we shall consider, "behavior modification," has been implicit in the preceding two sections on motivation and productivity. Rooted in the work of B. F. Skinner (1953) and many others, behavior modification involves rewards for desired behaviors and the withholding of rewards for undesired behaviors. Using this system, a manager rewards workers for each task they successfully complete. The rewards must immediately follow the completion of the task and must be desirable to the workers. Behavior that is unwanted is allowed to "extinguish" by not being rewarded. The rewards that follow the desired behavior tend to strengthen ("reinforce") that behavior so that it will be "learned" and become a part of the workers' behavioral repertoire. Instead of criticizing poor performance, a manager using this technique would let a poorly executed task pass and wait to reward one that is well done. Once behavior seems to be learned it does not have to be rewarded every time it occurs, but it must be rewarded occasionally so that it will not extinguish. To improve productivity a manager should make a big to do when weekly or monthly goals are reached and remain silent when goals have not been attained. Extensions of behavior modification in management can be seen in the considerable literature on incentive systems such as profit sharing and time off with pay.

One of the many problems with behavior modification is knowing which rewards are valued and which are not. Of course, everyone likes to be praised, but over a period of time rewards should be varied so as to retain their impact. Giving rewards that have little value to subordinates will not reinforce behavior and may make them feel exploited. Another problem with behavior modification is that the manager must be present and available to recognize and reward desired behaviors.

The three management techniques described above can be tremendously useful to a human services manager in spite of their many shortcomings. These techniques are not mutually exclusive; a manager may use all three at once. Job variety, monitoring goals and achievements, and rewarding good performance should be the concern of every manager even though these techniques may not be adopted in their entirety and followed to the letter.

PROFESSIONALS IN THE ORGANIZATION

A great deal of consternation in human services organizations stems from the tension created by professionals' wish for autonomy and organizations' demand for control (Finch, 1979; Wasserman, 1979). Another area that is problematic is the tug of war between an organization's requirement of loyalty to its authority and a professional's identification with his profession. These problems are compounded by the fact that many professionals in organizations have been led by their training and their professional associations to have high expectations in terms of salary, autonomy, fringe benefits, intellectual stimulation, and so on. These expectations may be inordinately high for many organizations, leading to more tension and frustration on the part of all involved. Such tension and frustration inevitably diminish productivity and interfere with an organization's progress toward its goals. In this section we shall examine the causes of these problems and try to find ways that managers can remedy them.

The original model of a professional, Daniels (1969) suggested, was that of "a free agent contracting to perform a service for his client" (p. 55). Today, however, professionals no longer practice only on their own. They are employed by public, nonprofit, and private organizations of all sizes. Indeed, most human services professionals such as teachers, nurses, social workers, occupational therapists, and public health physicians are employed by bureaucratic organizations. This situation has led many writers to delineate the characteristics of professionals. Schriesheim, Von Glinow, and Kerr (1975), in a review of the literature, listed six attitudes and behaviors associated with professionals that are accepted by most authors:

Expertise—Professionals possess special knowledge and skills.

Ethics—Professionals have an obligation to serve the public according to a code of ethics that includes:

    a. Neutrality and objectivity in dealing with clients.

    b. The application of generally accepted standards of practice.

    c. No emotional involvement with clients.

    d. Help to maintain the standards of the profession.

Collegial Maintenance of Standards—Because of their expertise, professionals feel that they should police their own standards. They chafe at the imposition of others' standards.

Autonomy—Professionals want to maintain self-control over work activity and decisions pertaining to work.

Commitment to Calling—Professionals have a sense of dedication to their careers.

Identification with the Profession and with Fellow Professionals—Professionals are loyal to their profession and professional colleagues and see their colleagues as important referents.

Filley, House, and Kerr (1976) have compared these six characteristics of professionals with seven characteristics of organizations (see Table 8–2) and have shown where conflict can, and often does, arise between professionals and the organizations that employ them.

Kouzes and Mico (1979) suggested another view of potential conflict in human services organizations. They noted that in human services organizations there are three domains—the policy domain, the management domain, and the service domain. The policy domain consists of an organization's governing board. The executive director and other management level personnel constitute the management domain. Professionals who serve clients and who feel they are capable of self-governance since they possess expertise in serving clients comprise the service domain. Each domain, according to Kouzes and Mico, operates by its own idiosyncratic principles, success measures, structural arrangements, and work modes. Differences among domains along these dimensions create disjunction and discordance. Figure 2–4 depicts the three domains and the features that characterize each. Domain theory was discussed in greater detail in Chapter 2.

If it is true, as the gospel writer tells us, that one cannot serve two masters (or three), then perhaps conflict between professionals and organizations will always be with us. What can be done about this situation? Green (1966) asserted that it is a professional's responsibility to reconcile within himself the demands of his profession and those of his organization. Lest human services professionals think they are alone in having to accommodate their autonomy, creativity, and energies to the demands and constraints of another order of things, consider the following:

- A young musician who must pay attention to the exact musical directions of a conductor.
- An innovative educator in a conservative school system.
- A humanistically oriented military officer.

The orientations of seemingly disparate callings can be combined and used to enhance each other. What is required is a willingness to be flexible. For example, it is not impossible for a humanistically oriented social worker to function effectively in a bureaucracy. Pruger (1978) suggested that one can learn to use a bureaucracy to *improve* services.

Finch (1979) observed that professional education encourages identification with a particular professional orientation. This causes tension both between the professional and the organization and among professionals of different disciplines within the same organization. Professionals must attempt to find common ground for cooperation in bureaucratic organizations if these organizations are to work effectively for their clients. Professionals must be willing to transcend professional boundaries rather than be paralyzed by them. In this regard, a manager in a human services agency

TABLE 8-2. Areas of Conflict between Professional and Organization

	PROFESSIONAL CHARACTERISTICS					
ORGANIZATIONAL CHARACTERISTICS	*expertise*	*ethics*	*collegial maintenance of standards*	*autonomy*	*commitment to calling*	*external referents and identification*
bureaucratic authority and hierarchical control			conflict	conflict		
desire for loyalty to the organization		conflict			conflict	conflict
desire for professionals to adopt a managerial orientation					conflict	conflict
placement of employees into work groups				conflict		conflict
desire for secrecy		conflict		conflict		conflict
use of unscientific decision-making processes	conflict			conflict		
network of rules				conflict		

From *Managerial Process and Organizational Behavior*, 2nd edition, by A. C. Filley, R. J. House, and S. Kerr. © 1976, 1969 by Scott, Foresman and Company. Reprinted by permission.

that is interdisciplinary would do well to avoid overidentification with his own profession so that subordinates of other disciplines will not feel they are in the out-group. On the other hand, distancing oneself from one's profession may bring accusations from subordinates of the same profession that the profession is being sold out by the manager. This dilemma must be handled judiciously so as not to jeopardize interdisciplinary team building by covertly encouraging workers of different disciplines to rally around artificially disparate professional identities. This is not to suggest that all human services professionals are equipped to perform the same functions regardless of their knowledge and skills acquired through formal training. It is, however, to suggest that too much attention to specialization and professional differences can severely fragment a supposedly interdisciplinary staff. As Robinson (1979) observed, "Disciplines are intellectual conveniences, not sovereign states."

In order to help professionals adapt to the exigencies of organizations, managers should attempt to initiate discussions, in staff meetings and in individual supervision sessions, to explore the ways that reconciliations can be made among the three domains in human services organizations. It is imperative that managers come to grips with their own inner conflicts in this regard so that they can provide a role model for their subordinates. This is especially true in their role as buffer between the policy domain and the service domain. Managers must be able to make creative compromises in order to promote an environment in which professionals and the bureaucracy can be flexible and accommodate to each other.

This chapter has dealt with the issue of getting things done in an organization. In the next chapter we shall take up the problem of deciding whether what was done is what was intended and was done well.

REFERENCES

CAMUS, A. *Notebooks, 1935–1942*. New York: Knopf, 1963.

CARLISLE, H. M. *Management Essentials: Concepts and Applications*. Chicago: Science Research Associates, 1979.

DANIELS, A. K. "The captive professional: bureaucratic limitations in the practice of military psychiatry." *Journal of Health and Social Behavior* (1969) 10(4): 255–265.

FILLEY, A. C., HOUSE, R. J., AND KERR, S. *Managerial Process and Organizational Behavior*. 2d edition. Glenview: Scott, Foresman, 1976.

FINCH, W. A. "Social workers versus bureaucracy." In C. E. Munson (ed.), *Social Work Supervision*. New York: Free Press, 1979.

FRENCH, J. R. P., AND RAVEN, B. "The bases of social power." In D. Cartwright and

A. F. Zander (eds.), *Group Dynamics: Research and Theory*. New York: Harper, 1960.

GREEN, A. D. "The professional worker in the bureaucracy." *Social Service Review* (1966) 40(1):71–83.

HERZBERG, F., MAUSNER, B., AND SNYDERMAN, B. *The Motivation to Work*. 2d edition. New York: Wiley, 1959.

HOFSTEDE, G. H. "The colors of collars." *Columbia Journal of World Business* (1972) 7(5):72–78.

KOUZES, J. M., AND MICO, P. R. "Domain theory: an introduction to organizational behavior in human service organizations." *Journal of Applied Behavioral Science* (1979) 45(4):449–469.

LEVINSON, H. "Management by whose objectives?" *Harvard Business Review* (1970) 48(4):125–134.

LEWIN, K. *Field Theory and Social Science*. New York: Harper, 1951.

MASLOW, A. H. *Motivation and Personality*. New York: Harper, 1954.

McLAUGHLIN, C. P. "Productivity and human services." *Health Care Management Review* (1976) Fall:47–60.

PRUGER, R. "Bureaucratic functioning as a social work skill." In B. Baer and R. C. Federico (eds.), *Educating the Baccalaureate Social Worker*. Cambridge: Ballinger, 1978.

ROBINSON, P. Review of *Language and Responsibility* by Noam Chomsky. *New York Times Book Review* (1979) February 25:3.

SCHRIESHEIM, J., VON GLINOW, M. A., AND KERR, S. "The dual hierarchy: a review of the evidence and a theoretical alternative." In *Proceedings of the Twelfth Annual Conference*. College Park, Md.: Eastern Academy of Management, 1975.

SKINNER, B. F. *Science and Behavior*. New York: Macmillan, 1953.

VROOM, V. H. *Work and Motivation*. New York: Wiley, 1964.

WASSERMAN, H. "The professional social worker in a bureaucracy." In C. E. Munson (ed.), *Social Work Supervision*. New York: Free Press, 1979.

Evaluating Results

Human services organizations have a reputation for vaguely defined programs with no links to measurable outcomes and no apparent concern for their impact on the communities they purport to serve. According to this viewpoint, held by Demone, Schulberg, and Broskowski (1978), these programs operate far from public scrutiny and are run by managers who have neither the power nor the inclination to marshal resources to conduct formal program evaluations or to use whatever information they do have in order to make improvements. Recently, however, this situation has changed dramatically. Legislators, special interest groups, community leaders, and others in a position to loosen or tighten the strings of the public and private funding purses have demanded an accounting of the usefulness of human services programs. At first the questions to be answered are "What are we paying for? How many people are being served? What are the amounts of effort being expended per dollar of funding?" Later, the questions to be answered are "Does this program really work? Does it make a difference in its consumers' lives?" Old assumptions about the effectiveness of psychotherapy, prisoner work release programs, mass immunization programs, and a host of other human services have been challenged by those who fund them. Human services managers and administrators have resigned themselves to living in an "age of accountability." Some have grudgingly come to perceive real benefits in evaluating their programs. They have found that the information gleaned from formal program evaluations can be quite useful for internal program planning, budget preparation, quality assurance, resource allocation, management control, and decisionmaking. These managers, many of whom were accustomed to relying on their own informal observation as a major source of information, have come to accept what Attkisson, Brown, and Hargreaves (1978) called the basic tenet of program evaluation: "improvement through assessment."

I have perhaps idealized the manner in which managers have come to accept program evaluation. Indeed, many managers resist formal scrutiny of their programs for reasons we shall examine later in this chapter. Nonetheless, program evaluation is here to stay and managers must learn to live with it. This chapter will attempt to define program evaluation in human services. It will then move on to a discussion of the different levels and types of evaluation studies. Next will come an examination of how management and program evaluation can be integrated in a human services organization. Finally, the chapter will try to peer into the future of program evaluation in the human services. This will not be a "how to" chapter in the manner of the chapter on budgeting. Rather, it will attempt to introduce the new manager in the human services to the basic concepts and forms of program evaluation. Two excellent sources of information on how to carry out evaluation studies are Maanen (1979) and Attkisson, Hargreaves, Horowitz, and Sorensen (1978).

Before attempting to define program evaluation, we should pause to consider the importance of feedback for the human services organization. Feedback is, as we saw in Chapter 2, an essential component of any system and is the chief purpose of program evaluation. It is essential because it keeps the system focused on the core purpose, the purpose for which the system exists and which is consistent with its values.

It is useful to distinguish between negative and positive feedback as these terms are used in general systems theory. When we speak of feedback as having a correcting influence on a system we are really speaking of *negative* feedback. Negative feedback is the way in which a system says to itself, in effect, "We are not progressing toward our stated goals; we are off course. Changes must be made to put us back on course toward our goals." In this way, the system can adjust its activities and processes in order to set a more direct course toward what it originally set out to accomplish.

Positive feedback, on the other hand, gives the system the message that it is progressing toward its goals *even when it is not*. Systems have a natural tendency to deviate from their goals in response to influences from a variety of internal and external forces. This deviation is further amplified if the system has no mechanism to detect and evaluate progress toward its goals. A system that is governed only by positive feedback, not counterbalanced by negative feedback, will move over time further and further away from its original purpose. A system that becomes altogether governed by this "deviation-amplifying process" (Maruyama, 1963; Hoffman, 1971) is vulnerable to a loss of identity; therefore, its very existence is in jeopardy.

Consider, as an example, the situation of a social agency founded many years ago to provide counseling and prenatal care for young, indigent unmarried mothers. As the years go on the agency tries to be responsive to several actual or potential funding sources that may have competing interests in terms of what services should be offered by the agency and how those services should be delivered. After some time has gone by the agency finds itself providing public education about contraception and offering few direct services to young, indigent unmarried mothers. Suddenly, the funding source that had clamored for public education cuts its funding to the agency saying, "We wanted your program to offer contraception education because of your background in providing services to unwed mothers. But since you're doing very little of that now, we want to find a more appropriate agency to fund."

This example is perhaps somewhat contrived, but it does suggest what can happen to an organization that has no way of keeping in touch with its original core purpose and no way of altering its course toward goals in a way that protects its existence. Program evaluation, as a formal component of the organization, is the system's way of insuring negative feedback. This feedback will allow the system to change its course back toward its original goals. It also allows the system to reconsider its goals in view of the shifting sands of consumer demands, its resources, its value system, and competing internal and external programmatic demands.

WHAT IS PROGRAM EVALUATION?

Following the notion that program evaluation is a mechanism for negative feedback, Attkisson and Broskowski's (1978) definition is a good place to begin answering the question "What is program evaluation?" Program evaluation is:

1. A process of making reasonable judgements about program effort, effectiveness, efficiency and adequacy.
2. Based on systematic data collection and analysis.
3. Designed for use in program management, external accountability, and future planning.
4. Focuses especially on accessibility, acceptability, awareness, availability, comprehensiveness, continuity, integration, and cost of services. (p. 24)

According to this definition, program evaluation encompasses a range of activities, including needs assessment surveys, cost accounting, analyses of information regarding productivity, quality assurance efforts, and a variety of other techniques and methods that will be discussed shortly. Before proceeding, though, I must point out that program evaluation is not identical to scientific research. Although program evaluation often employs some of the procedures of scientific research, such as random sampling and statistical analysis, program evaluation operates within a different context to answer specific program and management related questions. Scientific research seeks to generate new knowledge. Research also operates in a longer time frame and requires far greater precision in terms of study design and analysis. While these distinctions may seem trivial, they can become quite important when evaluation results and recommendations are to be used for management decisionmaking or for answering to external constituencies. The time constraints imposed by the need to make decisions quickly or to answer constituencies when called upon to do so make approximate information far more useful than the precise, well-reasoned information generated by elegantly designed and tediously executed scientific research projects. As any manager knows from experience, decisions will be made with or without the maximum amount of relevant information. Program evaluation is therefore an internal management responsibility to which the program manager must be particularly attentive.

For the purposes of this chapter let us assume that program evaluation is a highly technical job performed by professional evaluators working in a specially designated unit within the human services organization. It is a staff unit or department to which line managers have access for routine information and special studies of their programs. As Blanton and Alley (1978) suggested, the manager must *ask the questions* and must participate in and facilitate the study's design as well as the collection of the data. He must then take some action on the original question even if he chooses to reject the evaluators' interpretations and recommendations. In the final analysis, the manager must decide, for he is not only an information processor (as we saw in Chapter 5) but also, in functional terms, a *decider*: in this role the manager will find program evaluation most useful.

As we shall see, there are many different types of evaluation studies. But it is important first to examine some of the elements that characterize most evaluations. The beginning step in any attempt to do program evaluation is to pose the question that must be answered. A manager may want to know about outcomes of a particular type of service model or about the efficiency index of an entire program or of individual workers. Whatever the question, it must be posed in a precise way. It is not enough to simply ask, "How is this program doing?"

A good way to avoid vague questions is to focus on the program's goals. What are the program's goals? Are the goals being met? If not, then for what reasons? For the purposes of an evaluation, goals must be expressed in a way that renders them measurable. "Do outpatients get better after being treated for ten sessions?" is less informative than "Is there an average difference in the outpatients' global adjustment rating before and after they are seen for ten sessions?"

There are a few problems with trying to measure the degree to which a program has accomplished its goals. One is that goals are often vaguely expressed, making their measurement quite difficult. Another problem is that one program goal may conflict with another one, which complicates the question of which part of the program to evaluate. For example, a mental health clinic may state as goals the reduction of emergency visits by 10 percent and the limitation of counseling to five sessions per client. But the decrease in available counseling hours may cause clients to make greater use of emergency services. Finally, goals may change over time in response to changes in the availability of resources, the interests and skills of managers and staff, and client demands. One must be sure that the goals that the program *says* it wants to accomplish are the goals toward which it has been working. In any event, even the preliminary process of examining and stating program goals can be quite beneficial to the program and its manager because it helps keep him from losing sight of objectives.

Systematic measurement is the next characteristic that most evaluation studies have in common. The manager, in collaboration with the evaluator, must decide what measures of his program he wants to consider. This decision will depend both on what the goals of the program itself are and the reasons for doing the evaluation. For example, a decision to study a hospital's physical therapy department could focus on determining staff productivity in relation to the number of stroke patients treated in a given time period. The measure used would be a simple ratio of staff hours to number of patients. But, if the decision is to focus on patients' outcomes, it would be important to measure, say, changes in the patients' range of motion in paralyzed limbs after a specified number of treatments.

Some method of collecting data is the next feature of an evaluation. Data are facts about clients, staff, services, and so forth. Data have no real meaning in and of themselves and must be compared, analyzed, and interpreted to yield useful information. One method of collecting data about a program is direct and systematic personal observation. A manager must facilitate an evaluator's access to the workings of the program so that he can observe them as closely as possible. Interviews and questionnaires are other methods of collecting data. Questionnaires afford anonymity and thereby encourage more open and honest answers to questions. Client records, productivity statistics, and case-by-case outcome scores are other sources of data for the evaluator.

Once relevant data have been collected, they may be analyzed using some standard or set of criteria. For example, the average length of stay on a hospital ward can be compared with state or national standards of length of stay for that type of ward. From this analysis, interpretations are made that attempt to answer the manager's original set of questions about the program. Not all analyses involve comparisons against normative standards, but they do involve some sort of comparison, say, before and after a given event among groups.

Finally, a good evaluation should include recommendations about a course of action. A quality assurance study that indicates specific deficiencies in the manner in which services are rendered could lead to a recommendation that service workers be given training to help them improve their knowledge and skills in the deficient area. The rest, as indicated earlier, is up to the manager. He must consider the evaluations's findings and choose whether or not to accept the recommendations as aids to the decisionmaking process.

Having defined program evaluation in general terms, it is now time to turn our attention to the various levels and types of program evaluations in the human services.

LEVELS AND TYPES

By now it should be clear that program evaluation in a human services organization covers a lot of ground, from internal management to external accountability. Attkisson, Brown, and Hargreaves (1978) have developed a useful scheme for conceptualizing the levels of program evaluation in terms of the purposes for doing evaluations. For a summary of the tasks associated with each level of evaluation, see the right-hand column of Table 9–1. The levels, which these authors view as "being naturally ordered on a developmental hierarchy" (p. 69) are (I) systems resource management; (II) client utilization; (III) outcome of intervention; and (IV) community impact. Before discussing each level at some length, a caveat by Attkisson, Brown, and Hargreaves is worth noting:

> Effective evaluation at a given level depends, at least to some extent, upon adequate initial mastery of the lower levels. (p. 69)

"Systems resource management" (level I) concerns basic standards of operation and the ways in which they are monitored. At this level, program goals and priorities are formulated in keeping with community needs, available resources, and the standards, rules, and regulations of funding and regulatory agencies. Also at this level, program goals and priorities are translated into measurable intervention strategies. When these initial steps are completed, preferably early in the development of the program, routine procedures for monitoring the program's operations should be developed so that errors and problems in the way the program works can be detected and remedied as quickly as possible. In this regard, the program's commitment to the community and its own aspirations must be kept in mind. Information generated by this level of operation will help the manager determine whether or not resource allocations are adequate to meet established objectives.

Examples of the many types of evaluations that are done at level I are demographic reports on clients served, assessments of the need and demand for services, measures of fiscal and human resources allocated to the program, cost-finding, and productivity reports such as the one presented in Table 8–1. (Bunker, 1978, has much to say about this basic level of program evaluation).

TABLE 9-1. Typical Management Tasks and Evaluation Activities at Four Progressively Evolving Levels of Evaluation Activity

Level of Evaluation Activity	Typical Management Tasks	Typical Evaluation Activities
I. Systems resource management	• Clarify organizational objectives • Develop program plan and budget • Establish lines of management responsibility • Obtain and maintain financial support • Allocate fiscal resources and staff effort • Coordinate personnel supervision • Establish new services and phase out existing services • Relate to community advisory groups • Meet external reporting requirements and program standards • Monitor income and expenditures • Establish fees and billing rates	• Review objectives and formulate indicators of attainment • Meet external reporting requirements • Clarify roles of evaluator and integrate with management tasks • Develop improved information capability and integrate data collection systems • Review mandated services or documented needs • Establish evaluation liaison with community advisory groups and evaluators from other organizational levels • Monitor staff effort and deployment of human, fiscal, and physical resources • Collaborate in establishment of a cost-finding system and determine unit costs of services • Provide effort feedback to management and service staff
II. Client utilization	• Make workload projections • Maintain efficiency of service delivery • Assure equity of service access • Assure appropriate client screening and treatment assignment • Assure adequate treatment planning • Assure appropriate service utilization and integration with other community services at the individual client level • Assure continuity of care • Establish quality assurance program	• Monitor unduplicated counts of clients served • Analyze caseloads and client flow • Compare client demographics to census data and high risk-need populations • Analyze reasons for premature dropout and under-utilization of services • Assist in installation of problem oriented client record and monitor service needs of clients • Provide technical support for utilization review and other quality assurance activities • Analyze continuity of care • Analyze costs per episode of care within specific client groups or service settings

III. Outcome of intervention

- Provide services acceptable to clients and referral sources
- Detect and correct grossly ineffective service activities
- Assure that services are generally effective
- Improve cost-effectiveness of services
- Reallocate resources to support and enhance most cost-effective services
- Communicate service effectiveness to funding sources and advisory groups

- Routinely monitor client status
- Study client and referral source satisfaction
- Study posttreatment outcomes
- Compare program outcomes to outcome norms
- Undertake comparative outcome experiments
- Do systems simulation and optimization studies
- Compare cost-outcomes of different approaches to service needs and establish cost-effectiveness of services
- Find cost-outcome per duration of problem or illness within specific client groups and/or service settings

IV. Community impact

- Participate in regional health planning
- Develop joint interagency services and administrative support systems
- Provide effective primary prevention and indirect services
- Collaborate in integration of services for multiproblem clients and stimulate effective interagency referral system

- Assess community needs
- Undertake incidence and prevalence studies
- Test primary prevention strategies
- Evaluate consultation and education services
- Participate in systematic regional need assessment
- Facilitate and provide technical assistance to citizen and consumer input to need assessment, program planning, and evaluation

From *Evaluation of Human Service Programs* edited by C. C. Attkisson, W. A. Hargreaves, M. J. Horowitz, and J. E. Sorenson. © 1978 by Academic Press. Reprinted by permission.

"Client utilization" (level II) is concerned with the nature and the extent of the organization's services to clients. It has as its basic premise the notion that activities must be visible to be governable. Each part of the service delivery process can be monitored in terms of five categories:

1. Appropriateness of client screening and case assignment.
2. Adequacy of service planning.
3. Appropriateness of continued utilization of services.
4. Continuity of service.
5. Accessibility of services to target populations.

In order to monitor these aspects of the human services program, evaluations at this level can include counts of clients served; analyses of caseloads in terms of client demographics compared with characteristics of high risk or target populations; analyses of referral patterns by source and type of problem, dropout rates, utilization of services by type of problem; and quality assurance activities.

This last example, quality assurance, has become increasingly important in recent years. Quality service, according to Donabedian (1966), can be categorized in the following three-part framework:

a. Structure—organizational aspects that affect services, such as record systems, qualifications of service staff, physical plant, staff-client ratio.
b. Process—clinical procedures that constitute the actual service or care provided by the organization.
b. Outcome—the effect of the service or care.

Donabedian considers each of these aspects of quality service as necessary but not sufficient for quality care. Consequently, both he and Woy, Lund, and Attkisson (1978) have advocated a quality assurance program that integrates these three parts of the definition of quality care (Woy and co-workers discuss at length quality assurance in the context of program evaluation in the human services).

"Outcome of intervention" (level III) overlaps with the quality assurance efforts just mentioned in that its chief concern is how well the program works. This level goes beyond the efforts subsumed under level II in that it examines organizational effectiveness whereas quality assurance efforts are most often concerned with service effectiveness as it applies to a specific group of clients with specific problems. Evaluations at this level would be concerned with such matters as comparisons of several interventions or programs to determine which are most or least effective. This could be done by examining Kiresuk and Lund's (1978) goal attainment scale. A program's outcomes could also be compared with normative standards developed by researchers who have studied outcomes of similar treatment programs elsewhere.

The last level of program evaluation in the Attkisson, Brown, and Hargreaves (1978) scheme is "community impact" (level IV). Although this level is the least technically developed, it is the most important from a political point of view. In the first three levels evaluation studies look at specific questions:

What is being done?
Who is doing it?
How is it being done?
How well is it being done?
Does it work?

Level IV extends the last question, focusing on the broad effects of a program on an entire community. Taxpayers and their legislators, after sinking billions of dollars into health and social welfare programs, are beginning to ask how such programs affect society at large. Answers must be increasingly precise in future years both in order to justify current funding and in order to assist in planning for future services as available funding shrinks. Evaluations at this level examine community needs, prevention efforts, and the incidence of certain problems in a community.

Just as each of these levels depends on the one that precedes it, the effectiveness of evaluation at *all* levels depends on the organization's ability to gather, store, retrieve, and analyze information and on the role of the evaluator and his place in the organization. Since these topics are beyond the scope of this volume, the reader is referred to Attkisson, Hargreaves, Horowitz, and Sorensen (1978) and to Broskowski and Attkisson (1981).

THE MANAGER-EVALUATOR COALITION

The case for a close working relationship between human services management and program evaluators was made by Attkisson, Brown, and Hargreaves (1978):

> We shall continue to see poorly administered programs and disregarded evaluative findings *until* the self-evaluating organization becomes a reality and there is day-to-day working integration of administration and evaluation fully using the organization's evaluative capability. (p. 83)

The manager who relies only on hunches and personal observations for planning and decisionmaking is taking serious risks with the well-being of his program and its clients. At best his hunches may be incomplete; at worst they may be wrong. The problem of the underutilization of evaluative findings has received a good deal of attention in the literature on program evaluation (Cox, 1977; Davis and Salasin, 1975). However, there is relatively little in the human services management literature on what managers can do to make better use of evaluative studies (Broskowski, White, and Spector, 1979). A review of the parallels between the columns of Table 9-1 will be instructive in this regard.

Managers often criticize evaluators for producing studies that are too late with too little usable information. One also frequently hears managers complain that program evaluations are too densely written as well as too full of complex and irrelevant statistics. While these criticisms may in some cases be valid, the manager shares a large part of the responsibility to educate the evaluator in the way that studies should be packaged and presented in order to maximize their utility. As mentioned earlier, the manager must let the evaluator know what he needs in the way of information. An analogy can be made to the relationship between a program manager and the personnel director when a position in a program becomes vacant. The personnel director does not send over anyone he pleases to be interviewed by the program manager. Neither does the personnel director make the final decision about whom to hire. Rather, the program manager, who is a line manager, gives the personnel director, who is a staff manager, specific information about the kind of person he wants to be recruited for the vacant position. In short, the program manager makes a specific request of the personnel director, and the personnel director makes every effort to comply. Given the assumption that the program manager knows best the kind of person he needs to work in his unique program, how can it be otherwise? So it is with program evaluation. The manager must specify his needs, his problems, and, finally, his request for information. The program evaluator must deliver the information in a way that complies with the program manager's request.

In order for managers and program evaluators to work closely together, they must understand each other's working style and needs. This means a cordial working relationship between them. Once this relationship is formed, the manager must help the evaluator gain access to the line workers, who are important people in the conduct of an evaluation; without their cooperation data collection will be impossible. The manager must also educate the evaluator about how he approaches his work. He must help the evaluator understand that management work is characterized by complexity, an unrelenting pace, ambiguity, an action orientation, and fragmentation (Mintzberg, 1973). These characteristics have important implications for the manner in which evaluations should be carried out and how the findings should be presented. Essentially, the manager must help the evaluator see that brevity is paramount. This means that studies must meet what may seem to be unreasonable deadlines. Also it means that if the reports are not oral, they should be written in summary form and clearly headlined so as to highlight the most important information.

The anxiety that evaluations often engender suggests another major area of action for the manager in his alliance with the evaluator. The manager should see to it that line workers are kept informed and involved in evaluation efforts from beginning to end. Both the manager and the evaluator should meet with staff before any study is begun to explain the reasons for the study. This is especially important if the study is not routine. An early discussion about the reasons for doing a study and an explanation of the use that will be made of the findings will promote the staff's trust in the evaluator and will make them valuable resources as the study proceeds. In this regard, the manager's leadership is crucial, for if he resists the study, even in a subtle manner, so will his staff.

As the manager and the evaluator move forward with the study, the staff should again be consulted about their views on the questions to be examined by the evaluation. The opinions and perspectives of all workers, including secretaries and other support staff, will add a dimension to the study that the manager may not be able to supply.

In order to guarantee the highest quality evaluation through the cooperation of all workers and to promote an ethos conducive to future studies, the manager should be sure that studies look at program rather than individual outcomes. As suggested in Chapter 8, goals for entire programs should be set and their achievement measured publicly; individual goals and achievement should be the private business of the manager and each worker. If workers have reason to fear that their own shortcomings will be exposed by program evaluations, they cannot be expected to cooperate. Also, job security and salary should not hinge solely on program evaluation findings. Evaluation results should be only one source of information in decisionmaking and planning.

PROGRAM EVALUATION AND THE FUTURE

"Where professional testimonies once sufficed, there is now [and, we might add, will continue to be] a demand for accountability" (Webb, Henao, Johnstone, and Maxwell, 1977, p. 44). At the same time, increasing complexity in the political and professional aspects of human services delivery are being matched by an increasing awareness of systems concepts and computer technology as means to improve planning and management. The present and future manager in the human services must keep abreast of developments in the field of program evaluation not so that he will be able to conduct evaluations single-handedly but so that he will know what is available to him in the way of evaluation information. He must also know how to use such information as he pursues his complex career in human services management.

In order to keep abreast of developments in the field of program evaluation the manager should keep an eye on three areas within the field (Hargreaves and Attkisson, 1978). The first concerns the tools of the trade, the foremost of which is computer technology. Many clinical managers have the fantasy that computers are beyond human understanding except for those possessed of Einsteinian analytical and mathematical abilities. In challenging this fantasy—and it is only a fantasy—I hasten to suggest that a manager does not necessarily need to know how to program or operate a computer, much less understand how one actually works. A competent program evaluator should be able to do that. The manager should have an understanding of what a computer can and cannot do in supplying information. The future will undoubtedly involve computers more in our daily work. Increasing sophistication (and, paradoxically, simplication from the user's point of view) in computer technology will enable an evaluator to produce almost unlimited combinations of data to respond to precise and complex questions from management. To learn more about computer technology and what may lie ahead, the reader should consult Broskowski and Attkisson (1981), Madnick (1977), and Martin (1976). Another way to learn about the capabilities of modern computers is to visit an electronics store for an equipment demonstration.

The second area that must be monitored is the ever changing requirements for accountability. Since Senator Robert F. Kennedy championed requirements for formal evaluations of federally funded educational programs in the mid-1960s accountability has been an important part of the human services scene. Hargreaves and Attkisson (1978) predicted that the future will see highly integrated human services delivery systems working toward regionally defined goals and service priorities. The attainment of these goals will be monitored according to regional standards with common definitions of service units. The focus of accountability, according to these authors, will be the four levels of evaluation discussed earlier in this chapter. They also predicted that a national standard setting commission for human services (analogous to the present-day Joint Commission for the Accreditation of Hospitals) will provide public and private funding sources with information about every human services agency that receives public funding or insurance payments. The program manager, working closely with the evaluator, will have to monitor these trends and plan, manage, and evaluate programs according to emerging regional and national standards. Many other demands for accountability from government regulatory agencies and citizen groups will tax the manager's ability to provide information about program effectiveness. Advance knowledge of these demands will allow the manager to set the stage for gathering the appropriate information.

Finally, the manager must be aware of changes in the education of future evaluators. Hargreaves and Attkisson (1978) predicted that training programs will graduate evaluators with a variety of backgrounds and a wide range of skills. Conversance in this area will give the manager an added edge in recruiting an evaluator who is most able to meet the unique needs of his program for evaluation.

The preceding three chapters, on planning, budgeting, and implementing a program, taken with this chapter constitute a whole. They have been presented separately to allow for an examination of the highlights of each part. However, this fragmentary presentation is an artificial construction. A more accurate picture of the life of a human services program would show the elements of planning, budgeting, implementation, and evaluation in a seamless dynamic interaction, each giving substance and meaning to the others. Such a view would help us appreciate the complexities and ambiguities of organizational processes and change. A statement by Emery and Trist (1965) gives us a glimpse of this internal dynamic process in the context of the external environment:

> The main problem with studying organizational change is that the environmental context in which organizations exist are themselves changing, at an increasing rate, and towards increasing complexity. (p. 21)

REFERENCES

ATTKISSON, C. C., AND BROSKOWSKI, A. "Evaluation and the emerging human service concept." In C. C. Attkisson, W. A. Hargreaves, M. J. Horowitz, and J. E. Sorensen (eds.), *Evaluation of Human Service Programs*. New York: Academic, 1978.

ATTKISSON, C. C., BROWN, T. R., AND HARGREAVES, W. A. "Roles and functions of evaluation in human service programs." In C. C. Attkisson, W. A. Hargreaves, M. J. Horowitz, and J. E. Soresen (eds.), *Evaluation of Human Service Programs*. New York: Academic, 1978.

ATTKISSON, C. C., HARGREAVES, W. A., HOROWITZ, M. J., AND SORENSEN, J. E. (eds.). *Evaluation of Human Service Programs*. New York: Academic, 1978.

BLANTON, J., AND ALLEY, S. "How evaluation findings can be integrated into program decision making." *Community Mental Health Journal* (1978) 14(3):239–247.

BROSKOWSKI, A., AND ATTKISSON, C. C. *Information Systems for Health and Human Services*. New York: Human Sciences Press, 1981.

BROSKOWSKI, A., WHITE, S. L., AND SPECTOR, P. "A management perspective on program evaluation." In H. C. Schulberg and J. Jerrell (eds.), *The Evaluator and Management*. Beverly Hills: Sage, 1979.

BUNKER, D. R. "Organizing evaluation to serve the needs of program planners and managers." *Evaluation and Program Planning* (1978) 1(2):129–133.

COX, G. B. "Managerial style: implications for the utilization of program evaluation information." *Evaluation Quarterly* (1977) 1(3):499–508.

DAVIS, H. R., AND SALASIN, S. E. "The utilization of evaluation." In E. L. Struening and M. Guttentag (eds.), *Handbook of Evaluation Research*. Beverly Hills: Sage, 1975.

DEMONE, H. W., SCHULBERG, H. C., AND BROSKOWSKI, A. "Evaluation in the context of developments in human services." In C. C. Attkisson, W. A. Hargreaves, M. J. Horowitz, and J. E. Sorensen (eds.), *Evaluation of Human Service Programs*. New York: Academic, 1978.

DONABEDIAN, A. "Evaluating the quality of medical care." *Milbank Memorial Fund Quarterly* (1966) 44(3):166–206.

EMERY, F., AND TRIST, E. "The causal texture of organizational environments." *Human Relations* (1965) 8(1):21–32.

HARGREAVES, W., AND ATTKISSON, C. C. "An evaluator of the future." *Evaluation and Program Planning* (1978) 1(2):141–144.

HOFFMAN, L. "Deviation-amplifying processes in natural groups." In J. Haley (ed.), *Changing Families*. New York: Grune & Stratton, 1971.

KIRESUK, T. J., AND LUND, S. H. "Goal attainment scaling." In C. C. Attkisson, W. A. Hargreaves, M. J. Horowitz, and J. E. Sorensen (eds.), *Evaluation of Human Service Programs*. New York: Academic, 1978.

MAANEN, J. V. "The process of program evaluation." *Grantsmanship Center News* (1979) January–February:29–74.

MADNICK, S. E. "Trends in computers and computing: the information utility." *Science* (1977) 195:1191–1199.

MARTIN, J. *Principles of Data-based Management*. Englewood Cliffs: Prentice-Hall, 1976.

MARUYAMA, M. "The second cybernetics: deviation-amplifying mutual causal processes." *American Scientist* (1963) 51:164–179.

MINTZBERG, H. *The Nature of Managerial Work*. New York: Harper & Row, 1973.

WEBB, L. J., HENAO, S., JOHNSTONE, E. E., AND MAXWELL, R. L. "Introducing accountability in an outpatient mental health clinic: an administrative process evaluation." *Administration in Mental Health* (1977) 5(1):44–54.

WOY, J. R., LUND, D. A., AND ATTKISSON, C. C. "Quality assurance in human service evaluation." In C. C. Attkisson, W. A. Hargreaves, M. J. Horowitz, and J. E. Sorensen (eds.), *Evaluation of Human Service Programs*. New York: Academic, 1978.

10 Personnel Management

Those functions of organizational life that involve the staffing of the enterprise can become the subject of debate and heated disagreements in many settings. This is all the more true in human services agencies, which have highly educated work forces with egalitarian ideals that may make the manager-worker relationship problematic. In most human services organizations it seems that everyone has a strongly held opinion about how to classify jobs, what the specifications and qualifications for a position should be, how to recruit and hire for the position, and even what title the new person should have. Moreover, many people in human services organizations have something to say about how they are oriented to their jobs and how they are supervised, evaluated, and compensated for their work. The manager's actions regarding these issues can be, and often are, the source of untold grief for all concerned. What is variously referred to as human resource management, staffing, the employment function, and personnel management is a veritable mine field for both the new and the experienced manager. Furthermore, the arrangement of the mines in every organization is different and the ways in which they explode vary from one organization to another. It is ironic that although 60 to 80 percent of the costs of most human services agencies are personnel costs, personnel issues are typically the least well understood by managers. This chapter will help guide the new manager through the personnel mine field.

Many "people problems" will inevitably block the path to excellence in an organization, regardless of the effort put into planning and coordinating. The manager must try to prevent these problems by hiring the most mature, adjusted, and skilled employees, and he must know how to identify problems early and work with employees to improve a troublesome situation as rapidly as possible. To that end, this chapter will begin with a basic

concern of personnel management: designing positions, including the determination of minimal qualifications and responsibilities. We will then discuss recruiting and hiring. The third section will consider the manager's interaction with an employee who has been hired, including such issues as
orientation and supervision. The performance appraisal function is discussed
next. Then there will be an examination of some of the considerations involved in incentives and rewards. Finally, we will discuss how to handle unsatisfactory performance.

Before proceeding, two assumptions must be stated. One is that the
manager works in an organization large enough to have a personnel department. The other is that the organization has a set of published personnel
policies and procedures that are available to every employee and are updated regularly. These assumptions will keep our discussion within the
scope of this book. They are also useful in that effective personnel management in organizations that have personnel departments is dependent largely
on the quality of the working relationship between the program manager
and the director of the personnel department. A manager who does not
have access to a professional personnel director will have to undertake a
more detailed study of these issues than can be supplied here.

JOB DESIGN

The logical way to begin an introduction to personnel management is to
discuss how jobs are designed. To do that we must go back to a theme
that has appeared throughout this book: the goals of the organization. In
order to know how work should be delineated, it is first necessary to know
what the organization or program seeks to accomplish. A clear statement of
the program's purpose can be derived from planning documents, grant proposals, funding agency board meetings, and memorandums from funders
and top administrators. Once these issues are clear we have the foundation
for staffing the program. Metzger (1975) suggested fourteen distinct pieces
of information that the job designer should have about a proposed job:

1. The objective of the job, including its basic mission and what it
   accomplishes;
2. To whom the incumbent reports;
3. How many people he supervises;
4. What level and types of positions report directly to the incumbent;
5. Which areas and operations are involved directly in the position;
6. To what extent the incumbent is responsible for actions and decisions,
   completely or partially;
7. Whether his actions are subject to approval from his supervisor;
8. The extent to which he is responsible for results;

9. The type of planning involved in the job;
10. Other units of the institution which are directly affected by this planning;
11. The relationships of the incumbent in the job to other departments within the institution and others outside the institution;
12. The extent and nature of his responsibilities for policy interpretation;
13. The procedures and methods to be followed;
14. Specialized technical information required to handle the job. (p. 51)

With these questions in mind the manager can proceed through the five phases of designing a job. The first, quite simply, is to name it. Job titles are not only useful descriptions of the position; they are also highly valued "ego" factors for the incumbents. Applicants for jobs are often as interested in the title of a position as they are in the salary it carries. But, titles should accurately describe the position and should not be misleading. This first phase, called "job identification," requires the manager both to name a position and to assign it a position number. Of course, job identification practices vary from one organization to another.

The preparation of a "job summary" is the second phase of job design. This summary is a brief and general decription of what the job holder must do on the job. It is used in recruiting and in grouping similar positions into classifications (to be discussed subsequently). The job summary also differentiates each job to be performed in the same program.

A "job duties statement" constitutes the third phase of designing a job. This phase is really the cornerstone of the formal job description (see Figure 10–1). It deals with each duty of the incumbent as specifically as possible. It also deals with how and why each duty is to be performed. The job identification, job summary, and job duties statement document what is expected of each incumbent. They constitute the standard against which performance is measured after a short probationary period and on each incumbent's anniversary of hiring.

The fourth phase of job design is the preparation of the "job specification," which delineates the exact requirements for doing the job. This statement should cover the educational background and skills required, the types of problem-solving skills required, to whom the incumbent will be accountable and who will be accountable to him, and the physical demands and working conditions of the job. Equal Employment Opportunity Commission (EEOC) regulations stipulate that job requirements be specifically related to job duties. For example, a college degree cannot be required if it is clearly not necessary to do the job in question. The job specification is an important document that serves as a shopping list during the recruiting process. It gives the personnel director and his staff the information they need to screen resumés in the early stages of searching for candidates. Figure 10–2 is an example of a job specification.

FIGURE 10-1.   Job Description

JOB IDENTIFICATION

Job Title: Intake Clerk   Department: Central Intake

Job Code: 06249-01

Date: May 13, 1980

Description prepared by: J. Thomas

JOB SUMMARY

Determines eligibility for program of all applicants for services and completes all intake paperwork prior to clients' being seen by professional staff.

JOB DUTIES

1. Greets each new applicant for services in the program.

2. Interviews each prospective client to determine eligibility for services according to the guidelines provided.

3. Reads administrative memoranda to keep informed about changes in eligibility criteria.

4. Prepares monthly statistical report on the demographic characteristics of all clients meeting eligibility criteria.

5. Sends letters to referral sources informing them on action taken on the clients referred to the program.

6. Does routine typing, filing, and telephone answering in the Central Intake Office.

The final phase of job design is usually a joint venture between a program manager and the personnel director. This phase involves placing the new position in a "job classification," which is a grouping of jobs with similar qualifications in order to standardize performance requirements and salary levels throughout the organization.

The five phases of job design may seem excessively detailed to suit most human services managers. However, the effort put into documenting precisely what a job is, how it should be done, and who is qualified to do it will help the manager avoid the many problems that arise when workers are hired with an inadequate understanding of what a job entails. The human services job market is often inflated with overqualified people eager to accept positions they only half understand. Moreover, managers are often eager to fill vacancies before positions are eliminated or before a truly attractive candidate gets away. Failure to communicate all pertinent information about a position before it is filled many turn the early enthusiasm of

FIGURE 10-2.   Job Specification

JOB IDENTIFICATION

Job Title: Pediatric Nurse Specialist   Department: Migrant Worker
                                                             Outreach Program

Job Code: 82274-02

Date: January 23, 1980

Description prepared by: H. Schubert

JOB SPECIFICATIONS

Education:	B.S. and M.S. in nursing with special emphasis in pediatrics; additional course work in neonatal care, nutrition, and psychiatry.
Experience:	One year of post-master's work, preferably in a neighborhood health center or outpatient clinic. Must be able to perform physical assessments on children of all ages and provide preventive health care counseling to indigent families. Must be able to work autonomously in the field.
Accountability:	Will supervise one L.P.N. and one health technician. Will report to the Director of the Migrant Worker Outreach Program.
Physical Demands:	Good health to meet the demands of frequent travel in rural areas on poor roads.
Working Conditions:	Seventy-five percent of working time will be spent in field visiting migrant worker families. Remaining time will be spent in clinic at Migrant Worker Health Center. Outdoor working conditions can be unpleasant, particularly during summer.

both the hasty manager and the eager candidate into bitter disappointments when misunderstandings surface later.

RECRUITING AND HIRING

Personnel management, like so many other aspects of management, is affected by the external constraints imposed by governmental agencies, laws, and labor unions. Before beginning a discussion of recruiting and hiring I would suggest that one of the most important and far-reaching of these laws is Title VII of the Civil Rights Act of 1964, which established the Equal Employment Opportunity Commission. The EEOC is responsible for eliminating discrimination based on age, sex, religion, race, color, and national origin. A manager should be sensitive to this and other legislation whenever any personnel action is contemplated. Managers should be aware of and conversant with agency policies regarding affirmative action, hiring of handicapped persons, and agency-union relationships.

Vacancies occur continually in organizations as a result of voluntary and involuntary terminations, transfers, organizational growth, promotions, retirements, sick leaves, leaves of absence, and other reasons. These vacancies burden the manager with the arduous task of recruiting and hiring staff, reducing both his own and the entire program's productivity until well after new personnel are on board. The negative effects of personnel vacancies sometimes induce managers to go to great lengths to keep employees, regardless of their performance. Similarly, marginal employees often manipulate managers with threats of quitting. It is important for a new manager to develop a thick skin about employee turnover. Turnover is a natural and inevitable phenomenon and, if not excessively rapid, a healthy opportunity for the program to replenish its ranks with new people full of new ideas and energy. On the other hand, of course, too much turnover is terribly disruptive. Excessive turnover can be avoided if employees are made to feel that they and their work are valued by the organization.

As the manager approaches the process of recruiting and hiring, he should be aware of his organization's procedure for filling positions, particularly in terms of what the proper relationship among himself, the applicant, and the personnel director should be. Many agencies subscribe to the theory of decentralized screening of applicants and centralized hiring. This means that the personnel department has the responsibility to do the initial screening of all applicants; the manager, responsibility to interview foremost contenders for a position and make the final hiring decision, subject to top administrative approval. The manager would do well to make sure he understands whether top administration typically grants approval as a formality or whether management insists on interviewing the candidate of choice.

For many managers, the temptation to bypass the personnel department and handle all phases of recruitment is great. For numerous reasons it is usually a grave error to succumb to this temptation. First, and most simply, it is easier to let the personnel department do the detailed work of sorting through a huge pile of resumés and applications. Second, the personnel department is in a better position than the manager to insure that fair hiring practices are followed and carefully documented. One of the most important reasons, however, is that management interference in personnel procedures usually leads to a messy situation in which both parties work at cross-purposes, with the job applicants caught in the middle. Such circumstances create confusion and hard feelings in all who are involved and often serve merely to delay further the hiring of a qualified applicant and prevent future harmonious relationships between the program and the personnel department.

Although the personnel department is responsible for the actual process of recruiting applicants for vacant positions, the manager will be involved in the process and should know something about how it works. It begins with the manager's giving the personnel department a detailed and complete picture of the kind of person he wants for the job. The manager should provide the personnel department with a job description and specifications and any other information that would help them recruit the kind of person best suited for the vacancy.

The search for candidates for a vacant position may begin within the organization itself. Indeed, many organizations have career ladders that allow people to move up through the ranks to higher paying, more responsible positions. It is generally good policy to promote from within in order to build incentives for good performance into the work system. But the organization that purports to have a career ladder and consistently hires outsiders will have a major morale problem. A career ladder that is a sham is worse than no career ladder at all. Townsend (1970) suggested that very few people really look ready and able to move up to a bigger job. He went on to say:

> I use the rule of 50 per cent. Try to find somebody inside the company with a record of success (in any area) and with an appetite for the job. If he looks like 50 per cent of what you need, give him the job. In six months he'll have grown the other 50 per cent and everybody will be satisfied. (p. 138)

If internal recruiting is to be done *before* external recruiting, one should be careful that the agency sanctions this method of recruiting and that no civil service, affirmative action, or union rules prohibit this method.

When it is impossible to fill positions from within the organization, the recruiting effort must turn to external candidates. Potential candidates from outside the organization can be recruited in a variety of ways. One way, popular in many organizations, is word-of-mouth recruiting by which employees tell their friends about openings for which they may be qualified. Outstanding workers often have outstanding friends who would be able to make significant contributions to the program. This type of recruiting is one in which a manager can play an active role as he encourages certain employees in the organization to spread the word about a particular vacancy. This method, however, should not be used in place of other methods of recruiting. Rather, it should be used in addition to other methods in order to avoid EEOC violations.

Another type of recruiting effort is to examine resumés and job applications that have come into the personnel department during the preceding three or four months. These files often turn up qualified candidates still available for employment. This type of recruiting can be done quickly; it is inexpensive; and it creates goodwill among those who learn that the organization does not file unsolicited resumés in the wastebasket.

When the foregoing methods fail to turn up qualified candidates, advertising is the best course to follow. Some agencies advertise all positions as part of their affirmative action plans. Advertising can be done in many creative ways that will increase the chances of recruiting the best person for the job. For instance, advertisements can be placed in professional journals and in newspapers in cities known to have a surplus of professionals in the field in which the vacancy exists.

During the recruiting process the manager should be aware of any affirmative action policies and procedures that apply to his agency. This issue will not be covered here because not all agencies are affirmative action agencies and because affirmative action rules change so often.

Once the personnel department has screened the applications and resumés, those that fit the specifications outlined by the manager should be sent to him for review. The manager should choose the three or four contenders who appear to be best qualified and arrange for interviews. Candidates should be interviewed by several people in the organization, including the manager himself, two or three people who would be the candidate's peers in the program, and the personnel director. This process gives the manager more information upon which to base a hiring decision and gives the candidate an opportunity to determine whether he would want to work in the agency.

The interview allows the manager to establish personal contact with each applicant and fill in the blanks in the resumé. It is an opportunity to ask about time gaps in the person's employment history and to find out about the exact nature of the person's education and work experience. It is also a chance to find out about the person's attitudes toward work and about his short- and long-range career goals. The interview should cover six general areas:

1. *Work History*
   Check dates of previous employment, account for gaps; reasons for leaving each job; attitudes about previous jobs and supervisors.
2. *Educational Background*
   Check dates and gaps in chronology; determine exact nature of training with its strengths and weaknesses; secure written permission to check degrees and schools attended.
3. *Outside Activities*
   Hobbies, recreational interests, community involvement, reading habits, and other indicators of the applicant's personal qualities.
4. *Ideas about Vacant Position*
   Applicant's ideas about how he would perform in the vacant position and how the job would relate to immediate and future goals.
5. *Self-assessment by Candidate*
   Candidate's assessment of own strengths and weaknesses and ideas about self-development in weak areas.
6. *Overview of Agency and Program*
   Manager's description of agency and program philosophy and goals;

description of the expectations of future incumbent of position under discussion.

The interview should go through several stages designed to put the applicant at ease and then to draw him out on the points outlined above. It should begin with a warm-up stage during which the manager develops rapport with the applicant. The next stage should be to get the applicant to begin talking, perhaps on some aspect of his resumé. The manager should then carefully draw him out by directing his attention to the first four areas of the outline. After providing the information in the sixth part of the outline, the manager should ask the applicant whether he would care to ask any questions. The manager should avoid asking yes and no questions; he should also avoid revealing any of his own personal biases that would prompt certain responses from the applicant or make the applicant feel that prejudice exists. An excellent source of interviewing technique is Garrett (1972). Although this classic book has a clinical orientation, it can be studied with personnel interviewing in mind.

After the manager has interviewed all the candidates he should talk with the personnel director and other staff members to get their opinions about each applicant. These opinions are valuable sources of information about how each candidate may fit into the organization.

At this juncture in the hiring process the manager will typically have selected a candidate. Occasionally, however, he will be torn between two equally qualified individuals. This is the time to ask the personnel department to do a thorough check of the top condenders' references. (Of course, references should be carefully checked even if there is only one top contender for a position.) At least three references should be checked for each candidate, one of whom should be the person's most recent employer. If the candidate objects to having his most recent or current employer contacted, his reasons should be explored carefully. However, since it is crucial to contact the most recent or current employer, in the event that an applicant does not want his current employer to know he is job hunting, the employer should be contacted only if the candidate is the first choice for the position. If, after being told that he is the first choice, he still refuses to allow his present employer to be contacted, his candidacy should be reconsidered. References provide the manager with information that will assist him in the final selection and will help forestall wrong hiring decisions. References should be asked the nature of their relationship with the candidate and how long they have known him. If they were his former employers, they should be asked about the nature of the work he did and about his performance. They should also be asked why he left their organization and whether or not they would be inclined to rehire the candidate. An answer in the negative should be carefully explored. They should also be asked to make any comments about the candidate not covered in the questions previously asked. Finally, degrees and licenses should always be verified.

As in any decisionmaking process, the information gained from the manager's own interviews, from those of others in the organization, and from references should be evaluated in the context of all that the manager knows about each of the candidates. This information should be weighed against the information the manager has about the nature of the vacant position and the climate of the organization. It is rare to find a candidate with whom everyone is totally pleased or who is totally qualified for the position that is open. Under these uncertain circumstances the manager will have to rely upon his experience in hiring and upon good judgement. The final decision should never be rushed in an attempt simply to close the issue and get on with business. A hasty decision about hiring usually backfires, ultimately costing more time as well as causing more disruption and anxiety in the organization than a slow and deliberate hiring effort ever will. Another pitfall to avoid in hiring is filling a position with a person who is extraordinarily overqualified: an overqualified employee may quickly outgrow the job and become discontented.

The question of overqualification has another side. For one thing, overqualification is not an acceptable reason for denying employment according to EEOC. A more important consideration, however, is that some well-qualified people who are accustomed to very demanding positions may, for perfectly acceptable reasons, be genuinely willing to take a less demanding and lower paying position. For these people, a more relaxed life style is preferable to the prestige and pay of the high pressure positions for which they are qualified. Many of these people are capable of making significant contributions to an organization.

Once a decision has been made, an offer should be extended in writing to the person chosen for the job. The written offer should clearly outline the program's and the manager's expectations of the person in the job. The letter should also state the starting salary, the starting date, when the new employee will be formally evaluated, and when he can expect to be eligible for a raise. Written information about medical insurance, vacations, and other benefits should also be sent to the new employee at this time. The applicant should be asked to reply to the offer in writing.

ORIENTATION AND SUPERVISION

After all the time and energy that is usually put into the recruiting and hiring process it is curious indeed that so little is done to integrate new employees into the organization. New employees are often given little or no direction about how work is performed or what is expected of them and must go through the slow process of finding out for themselves how, when, why, and where things are done in the organization. Or they are thrown into the fray and given an enormous workload and nothing more in the way of direction. Either way, the new workers are lost and probably more than a little resentful that no one has taken the time to show them the ropes. Also, until new workers manage to find their way in the organization, they are not very productive and the quantity, and perhaps the quality, of services to clients suffers.

The personnel department should inform new employees about such matters as employee benefits, income tax forms, and salary administration practices. But it is the manager's responsibility to make new employees feel welcome and to see to it that someone properly orients them to the program. He should make a point of meeting individually with each new worker and clarifying the role of the new worker vis-à-vis his own role and those of the new worker's peers. An understanding between the manager and the new employee about the exact nature of their respective roles within the program will promote job satisfaction and the worker's feeling that his efforts will produce progress toward defined goals in the program (Aplander, 1979).

The manager should assign each new employee to a veteran of the program whose responsibility it is fully to orient the newcomer to the daily routine. Particular attention should be given to the idiosyncratic aspects of the program, such as how cases are assigned to professional workers and how client records are written, stored, and retrieved. The new employee should also be oriented to practices regarding lunch and coffee breaks and other informal aspects of the work environment. A one-to-one approach during orientation will enhance a new employee's integration into the program. Although some aspects of a new employee's orientation may be delegated, the manager should closely supervise the orientation process and keep in touch with the new worker. This will insure that the new employee feels connected to the rest of the program.

The orientation process is usually thought of as a time limited task for each new employee, ending a few days or weeks after the new arrival's first day at work. However, because of the constantly changing nature of modern human services organizations, it is useful to think of orientation as an ongoing process and as part of the regular administrative and clinical supervision of every worker. Changes in policies and procedures, service eligibility requirements, accountability practices, and the technology of service delivery make ongoing orientation of staff a vital task for managing personnel.

In order to be effective in this often neglected aspect of managing people, a manager would do well to approach orientation in an organized way. Otherwise, many of the myriad bits and pieces of information that should be passed on to staff either will be lost or will reach some workers and not others. There are many methods of organizing information for new employees. One method is to keep a list of the things that must be communicated to staff at the program's weekly staff meeting. As each item is read it is checked off. In a program that is staffed around the clock, such as a hospital ward or emergency telephone service, a looseleaf binder can be used as a "pass-on book" in which important new items for each shift are passed on. Memorandums and individual meetings with workers are also useful methods of ongoing staff orientation.

In any event, it is essential that the manager keep in constant communication with subordinates through weekly or at the very least biweekly staff meetings and through regular private meetings with each employee. It is easy to neglect these meetings when crises occur or when more attractive tasks present themselves. A manager who becomes so caught up with matters that divert attention away from the needs of subordinates for information, encouragement, direction, praise, and even humor will soon face a crisis of staff morale that will demand attention in a most unforgiving manner.

PERFORMANCE APPRAISAL

Workers' performance is continually appraised by everyone, but the various workers' managers have responsibility for formalizing this process in writing on an annual or semiannual basis. The formalization of appraisal guarantees that workers get an indication of how they are doing in their managers' eyes and what will be expected of them in the coming year. It is probably just as well that performance appraisals are required in a formal way each year since, according to Wexley (1979), most managers are ambivalent about doing them. Wexley suggested that managers feel that performance appraisal is something they should be doing both for the good of the organization and for the good of the workers. The information generated from this process is most useful for making decisions regarding promotions, transfers, and wage and salary administration. On the other hand, Wexley noted, they resent having to play God as they use rigid or ambiguous rating techniques to praise or criticize the personal worth of employees.

Employees, however, have a continuing need for information about the views their superiors have of them. They need to know what they are expected to do and whether they are perceived as meeting those expectations. Anxiety is generated in workers who do not get such information. In the same way, managers have a continuing need to let their subordinates know whether or not they are getting off the track in terms of personal and pragmatic goals and expectations.

So far, so good; performance appraisal is a good thing. But it is the written record and the forced-choice ratings required by many organizations that cause the problems in performance appraisal. A pragmatic approach to solving this is to face up to the fact that, however one looks at it, performance appraisal is subjective. Nevertheless, decisions about performance must be made. This requires managers to collect as much information as they can to assist in making performance appraisals (Kellogg, 1975). Even subjective evaluations of employees can be made against some standard of expected performance. The standard against which performance can be appraised should be contained in the job duties statement discussed earlier in this chapter. An essential element of these performance criteria is that they be clear. Also, performance criteria should be communicated to workers when they are hired so that they will not be surprised to learn about them later.

In actually doing performance appraisals, managers should take time to sit down with each worker to discuss all aspects of the worker's job and performance. The interview should be goal-oriented and designed to highlight areas for improvement. The performance appraisal interview should cover three general areas:

1. Personal characteristics such as initiative, leadership, and cooperativeness.
2. Job performance behaviors as they are delineated in the job duties statement.
3. Job results, including productivity and effectiveness.

After these areas have been covered, the appraisal should be carefully recorded on the forms required by the organization. Workers should be allowed to see their evaluations and to respond in writing to an evaluation with which they disagree.

One of the problems with performance appraisal is that the process can often degenerate into a barrage of criticism directed against the unfortunate employee. Meyer, Kay, and French (1965) pointed out that criticism by itself has a negative effect on performance. On the other hand, these writers suggested that mutual goal setting has a positive effect on performance and substantially reduces anxiety and defensiveness in the performance appraisal session. One should be careful, though, not to smother criticism with praise.

Managers faced with the difficult task of performance appraisal should beware of three common errors endemic to this process. The first is called the "leniency error"—rating everyone too high. The second is called the "central tendency error"—rating everyone the same. The third is called the "single trait (or halo) effect"—rating on the basis of the worker's best or worst trait without taking other behaviors and traits into account. These errors are particularly troublesome in that they reduce the usefulness of written performance appraisals in making decisions about promotions, transfers, special assignments, and raises in salaries.

The annual performance review is a good time to get employees' ideas on where they would like to go with their careers in the next year or two. This might involve an examination of responsibilities that could be added or dropped, as well as a discussion of how staff development efforts and current responsibilities would fit with future plans.

COMPENSATION AND BENEFITS

What is it that people want and expect from their work? Managers must know the answer to this question in order to be effective at providing proper compensation and incentives to subordinates. Lindahl (1949) asked a sample of workers to rank the things they wanted most from their jobs. He found that workers expressed the following wants and needs in this order of importance:

1. Full appreciation for work done.
2. Feeling "in" on things.
3. Sympathetic understanding of personal problems.
4. Job security.
5. Good wages.
6. Interesting work.
7. Promotion and growth in the organization.
8. Management loyalty to workers.
9. Good working conditions.
10. Tactful disciplining.

Because of the general economic decline of recent years, good wages and job security could be expected to be closer to the top of the list today. Nonetheless, this does not minimize the importance of the other worker needs and wants in the modern human services organization. Since Lindahl found that managers and nonmanagerial workers ranked these needs and wants quite differently, managers must be particularly attentive to the factors that concern workers. Managerial attention to all these factors is a central aspect of worker compensation for performance. Managers thus must constantly dispense informal rewards in the way of compliments, invitations to deliberate over problems requiring decisions, and sincere interest in workers as individuals. The human services manager should also be attentive to the desire of subordinates for professional growth and enhancement on the job and should strive to find ways to encourage and assist them.

As important as other factors are in compensating workers for their efforts, wages and benefits (e.g., medical insurance and vacations) are major aspects of personnel management and demand a great deal of managers' attention. Managers should be careful that all new employees are fully oriented to the specifics of wages and salaries and benefits. Moreover, managers should keep employees updated on changes in these plans and be able to answer any questions that may arise. Confusion about these aspects of organizational life can elicit highly emotional responses from employees.

Differences in pay for people with the same education and experience doing the same work within a program should be avoided. Most organizations have wage and salary and benefits plans, which should be closely followed in practice by managers. Adherence to these plans, even when it may seem desirable to deviate from them, will eliminate confusion and prevent hard feelings among employees.

UNSATISFACTORY PERFORMANCE

Welcome to the world of euphemism! No one likes to talk about such unpleasant matters as employees who are not performing satisfactorily and who may, when all else fails, have to be disciplined or fired. Consequently, a variety of terms, such as "marginal" and "unsalvageable," have been coined to describe the unsatisfactory worker. The euphemisms are indicative of the trouble most managers have with employees who simply are not doing their jobs or are performing poorly. The reluctance to come to grips with problem employees is especially widespread in the human services, where showing concern and understanding and giving people second chances (and third and fourth chances) are highly valued.

Important as these values may be to the ideological foundations of human services, managers must consider that limited resources do not allow us the opportunity to carry along workers who are unproductive or counterproductive. Managers confronted with workers' unacceptable behavior or performance should call the deficiencies to the workers' attention without delay. This should be done in private in a tactful and helpful manner; specific suggestions for improvement should be made. This approach is often enough to improve the situation by educating the worker.

When an informal and educational approach does not work and unsatisfactory performance persists, managers should consider writing a memorandum to the errant worker calling the problem to his attention and making specific recommendations for improvement. This memorandum should mention what has been done in the past by the manager and the worker to correct the problem. A written reprimand that becomes a part of the worker's personnel file does two things. First, it leaves no doubt in the worker's mind as to the seriousness and the possible consequences of his behavior. Second, it creates a record of the unsatisfactory performance and of attempts to remedy the situation should further action be required.

Written reprimands should certainly not be dispensed in a cavalier manner; they are serious black marks on workers' records. Nevertheless, their undesirability often so captures workers' attention that they dramatically improve their performance (and in some not so rare cases become model employees). When such changes do occur, new behaviors certainly speak louder than obsolete written reprimands in files. Moreover, when improvements persist, the written records can be altered to reflect the positive changes.

Occasionally, unsatisfactory behavior continues and can no longer be tolerated despite managers' best efforts to counsel and warn unsatisfactory performers. At other times a single action is so outrageous and harmful to clients, co-workers, and the organization that the risk of a second chance cannot be taken. In either of these unfortunate situations workers must be fired unless agency policy places constraints on the manager that prevent such action. Managers facing their first firings should enlist the help of a seasoned supervisor or colleague. The following are some useful steps to remember in firing errant workers.

First, never take any severe disciplinary action, such as terminating an employee, when angry. Anger clouds judgment and unjust and unfair actions that may be regretted later could be taken.

Next, the termination should be based upon a full investigation of all the pertinent facts and should conform to the organization's personnel policies. The reasons for the termination should be clearly documented for the record.

Third, the manager should meet with the worker at the end of the working day, preferably on a Friday, so that the terminated worker can save face with peers. The manager should conduct the interview in an unemotional and matter-of-fact manner by giving a brief sketch of the reason for the termination. The manager should then ask for the employee's resignation unless the reason for the termination warrants an immediate discharge. The manager should be prepared to answer the worker's questions about severance pay, accrued benefits, final working day, and expectations of the worker during the final days of work.

Finally, it is best to be sympathetic but firm and to limit the termination session to less than 45 minutes. Sessions that go on longer than 45 minutes usually become unbearably tense for both parties and inappropriately maudlin, with one party or the other saying things that will later be regretted.

Firings inevitably make other workers fearful and cause them to identify with the person who has been fired. Even when other workers know the reasons for the firing and agree that the action is necessary, they will rally around their fired colleague and treat him as a victim of a capricious and unreasonable manager. The manager will be treated quite coolly by all concerned for a week or two. This phenomenon almost always occurs when a person has been reprimanded, laid off, or fired; the manager should be prepared for it.

The manager should give other workers the reasons why the person was fired but should be careful not to reveal sensitive and private information about that employee.

Disciplining and firing unsatisfactory employees is probably the most anxiety producing aspect of managerial work, especially for human services workers, who are in the business of helping people. But these issues must be confronted if the service goals of the organization are to be accomplished. An excellent source for more information on this area is Steinmetz (1969). His chapter on firing is especially helpful. Also, as we saw earlier, colleagues and superiors should be consulted for assistance in difficult personnel issues. Personnel management is too complicated and the ramifications of improper action are too far-reaching for new managers to go it alone. When all else fails in the practice of personnel management, managers should consult the personnel department and the organization's personnel manual.

REFERENCES

APLANDER, G. G. "Role clarity and performance effectiveness." *Hospital and Health Services Administration* (1979) 24(1):11–24.

GARRETT, A. *Interviewing: Its Principles and Methods*. 2d edition. New York: Family Service Association of America, 1972.

KELLOGG, M. S. *What to Do about Performance Appraisal*. New York: Amacom, 1975.

LINDAHL, L. "What makes a good job." *Personnel* (1949) 25(4):263–266.

METZGER, N. *Personnel Administration in the Health Services Industry: Theory and Practice*. Holliswood: Spectrum, 1975.

MEYER, H. E., KAY, E., AND FRENCH, J. R. P. "Split roles in performance appraisal." *Harvard Business Review* (1965) 43(1):123–129.

STEINMETZ, L. J. *Managing the Marginal and Unsatisfactory Performer*. Reading: Addison-Wesley, 1969.

TOWNSEND, R. *Up the Organization*. New York: Knopf, 1970.

WEXLEY, K. N. "Performance appraisal and feedback." In S. Kerr (ed.), *Organizational Behavior*. Columbus: Grid, 1979.

APPENDIX
Learning Opportunities for New Middle Managers in Health and Human Services

There are many ways to obtain training in management skills. One can take courses in a graduate program in public health, social work, public administration, or education that has an emphasis on management. Colleges and universities frequently offer introductory courses in specific management skills such as planning, financial management, and personnel management. Numerous private and public institutes hold workshops and seminars that are an excellent source of continuing education. Also, the annual meetings of many professional organizations in the human services give workshops and lectures on management topics. Since the continuing education scene is constantly changing, the following list of learning opportunities for new human services managers will only be a representative sampling of what is available all over the United States. No such list could be exhaustive.

American College of Hospital Administrators
840 North Lake Shore Drive
Chicago, Illinois 60611

Conducts workshops and seminars; provides information about training programs in hospital administration; publishes a quarterly journal on health and hospital administration.

American Management Associations
135 West 50th Street
New York, New York 10020

Conducts workshops and seminars on management all over the country.

139

Applied Gerontology Certificate Program
San Francisco State University
1600 Holloway Avenue
San Francisco, California 94132

Gives courses in managing gerontology programs leading to a certificate.

Aspen Seminars
Aspen Systems Corporation
20010 Century Boulevard
Germantown, Maryland 20767

Offers seminars for health care managers on a variety of administrative topics, including financial management and nursing administration, in various locations throughout the country.

Association of University Programs in Health Administration
One Dupont Circle, Suite 420
Washington, D.C. 20036

Provides information about accredited graduate programs in health administration.

Center for Health Services Continuing Education
School of Public and Allied Health
University of Alabama at Birmingham
University Station
Birmingham, Alabama 35294

Offers graduate programs, courses, and self-study programs in health and mental health administration.

Center for the Study of Social Administration
School of Social Work
Hunter College
129 East 79th Street
New York, New York 10021

Conducts courses and grants a certificate in human services management.

College of Public Affairs
American University
Washington, D.C. 20016

Offers graduate programs and courses for certificates in public administration.

Continuing Education
Baruch College
17 Lexington Avenue
New York, New York 10010

Offers courses in accounting, computers, and other management topics.

Department of Health Administration
School of Public Health
University of North Carolina
263 Rosenau Building 201H
Chapel Hill, North Carolina 27514

Offers graduate programs and courses leading to a certificate in health administration.

Division of Community Psychiatry
School of Medicine
University of North Carolina
Building 208-H
Chapel Hill, North Carolina 27514

Conducts workshops in the development and management of mental health services.

Division of Continuing Education
Menninger Foundation
P.O. Box 829
Topeka, Kansas 66601

Presents courses and workshops for certificates in various aspects of mental health administration.

Doctoral Program in Social Policy and Social Work
Virginia Commonwealth University
Raleigh Building
Richmond, Virginia 23284

Offers a specialization in human services administration within the doctoral program.

Educational Research Center
New Mexico State University
Las Cruces, New Mexico 88003

Offers courses and a doctoral program in program evaluation in the human services.

Florence Heller Graduate School for Advanced Studies in Social Welfare
Brandeis University
Waltham, Massachusetts 02154

Offers a master's degree and several doctoral programs in health, mental health, and public service management and administration.

Graduate College
Golden Gate University
536 Mission Street
San Francisco, California 94105

Offers graduate programs in business, health services, and public administration at its main campus and at extension campuses on military bases across the country.

Graduate Field of Human Service Studies
Cornell University
N135 MVR Hall
Ithaca, New York 14853

Offers graduate programs and courses leading to certificates in human services management.

Graduate School of Management and Urban Professions
New School for Social Research
66 Fifth Avenue
New York, New York 10011

Offers courses and graduate programs in public services management.

Health Administration Education
University of Wisconsin
610 Langdon Street
Madison, Wisconsin 53706

Presents courses in health administration leading to a certificate.

Health Administration Program
School of Public Health
University of Minnesota
Minneapolis, Minnesota 55414

Offers graduate programs in health administration and a part-time program leading to a certificate in mental health administration.

Institute for Human Service Management
California State University
1401 21st Street, Suite 300
Sacramento, California 95814

Conducts courses leading to a certificate in human services management.

Joint Center for Human Services Development
School of Social Work
San Jose State University
San Jose, California 95192

Offers consultation and training in human services management leading to a certificate.

Learning Resources Corporation
8517 Production Avenue
San Diego, California 92121

Offers courses in management across the country.

National Training Laboratories
1815 North Fort Myer Drive
Rosslyn, Virginia 22209

Presents courses in group dynamics, leadership, and management.

Program of Continuing Education
School for Social Work
Smith College
Northampton, Massachusetts 01063

Offers summer courses in supervision and administration in social work.

Program Evaluation Master's Degree Program
Graduate School
Hahnemann Medical College and Hospital
230 North Broad Street
Philadelphia, Pennsylvania 19102

Offers a master's degree in program evaluation in the human services, with an emphasis on mental health.

School of Applied Social Sciences
Case Western Reserve University
Cleveland, Ohio 44106

Offers courses and graduate programs in human services administration.

School of Education
Boston University
232 Bay State Road
Boston, Massachusetts 02215

Offers graduate programs and courses in human services and educational administration.

School of Public Health and Tropical Medicine
Medical Center, Tulane University
New Orleans, Louisiana 70112

Offers graduate programs and courses in health administration.

School of Social Welfare
University of Kansas
Twente Hall
Lawrence, Kansas 66045

Conducts courses and graduate programs in human services management.

School of Social Work
Florida State University
Bellamy Building
Tallahassee, Florida 32306

Conducts graduate programs and courses in administration and program evaluation in the human services.

School of Social Work
Rutgers–The State University
New Brunswick, New Jersey 08903

Offers graduate programs and courses in human services management.

Southern Regional Education Board
130 Sixth Street, N.W.
Atlanta, Georgia 30313

Holds workshops throughout the South in management related topics in the fields of mental health and higher education.

Staff College
National Institute of Mental Health
5635 Fishers Lane
Rockville, Maryland 20852

Offers week-long courses in the development and management of mental health programs and in various management related topics such as program evaluation and client recordkeeping; also offers a year-long self-study course for mental health administrators; certificates are awarded.

University Associates, Inc.
8517 Production Avenue
San Diego, California 92121

Conducts a graduate program and courses leading to a certificate in management at various locations throughout the country.

Western Interstate Commission for Higher Education
P.O. Drawer P
Boulder, Colorado 80302

Conducts workshops and seminars on various topics in mental health and educational administration.

INDEX

DATE DUE

APR 1 8 1999